IN GOD'S HANDS

HOME TO HEATHER CREEK

IN GOD'S HANDS

Leslie Gould

Home to Heather Creek is a trademark of Guideposts.

Copyright © 2024 by Guideposts. All rights reserved.

This book, or parts thereof, may not be reproduced, stored in a retrieval system, or transmitted in any form or by any means, electronic, mechanical, photocopying, recording, or otherwise, without the written permission of the publisher.

The characters and events in this book are fictional, and any resemblance to actual persons or occurrences is coincidental.

Scripture quotations in this volume are taken from the *The Holy Bible, New International Version* (NIV). Copyright © 1973, 1978, 1984, 2011 by Biblica, Inc. Used by permission of Zondervan. All rights reserved worldwide.

Published by Guideposts
100 Reserve Road, Suite E200
Danbury, CT 06810
Guideposts.org

Cover by Lookout Design, Inc.
Interior design by Cindy LaBreacht
Additional design work by Müllerhaus
Typeset by Aptara, Inc.

ISBN 978-1-961125-29-2 (hardcover)
ISBN 978-1-961125-42-1 (epub)

Printed in the United States of America
10 9 8 7 6 5 4 3 2 1

Acknowledgments

Many thanks to the farmers in my life—Marva, Wally, Teresa, Calla, and Sam Walker. The wonderful times my family and I have spent with all of you over the years have found their way into all of my *Home to Heather Creek* novels and are embedded in our hearts. I'm grateful, also, for the inspiration I find through my relationships with my husband and four children. Through good times and hard times, I'm constantly learning what it means to be a family and those insights have found their way into this story. Writing for the *Home to Heather Creek* series has been an enjoyable, collaborative experience. I'm indebted to the other writers and to the editors, who have all made this project an imaginative success. It has been an absolute delight to be included in this series.

—Leslie Gould

Home to Heather Creek

Before the Dawn

Sweet September

Circle of Grace

Homespun Harvest

A Patchwork Christmas

An Abundance of Blessings

Every Sunrise

The Promise of Spring

April's Hope

Seeds of Faith

On the Right Path

Sunflower Serenade

Second Chances

Prayers and Promises

Giving Thanks

Holiday Homecoming

Family Matters

All Things Hidden

To Love and Cherish

A Time to Grow

Sentimental Journey

Helping Hands

Growing Pains

In God's Hands

IN GOD'S HANDS

Chapter One

The metal bowl heaped full of potato salad felt cool against Charlotte's lap as she rode with her husband, Bob, and her grandchildren into Bedford from Heather Creek Farm.

"Who else is going to be there?" twelve-year-old Christopher asked from the backseat of the king-cab pickup.

"Pete and Dana, of course." The barbecue was at the home of Charlotte and Bob's younger son, Pete, and his wife, Dana. "And Dana's parents." Bonnie and Chuck Simons visited often; at least Bonnie did.

"And Sam," sixteen-year-old Emily added in an authoritative tone. Sam would drive straight to the barbecue from classes at Central Community College in Grand Island.

Bob slowed at the city limits. "Is there a purpose for this get-together?"

"Not that I know of." Charlotte agreed a Tuesday evening family gathering was unusual, especially in September, but she hoped that Pete and Dana had a buyer for their house and this was to be a celebration. The workers who were building their new house on the farm needed to be paid before they continued, and even though it was hard to believe with the blisteringly hot weather, winter was not far away.

Bob turned off the highway onto Bayard Lane and down the tree-lined street, driving between houses built right after World War II during Bedford's last building boom. Bob parked in front of a FOR SALE sign that was staked into the strip of grass between the sidewalk and yard in front of the two-story cottage. There was no SALE PENDING strip on it, no indication there might be a buyer. "Pull forward," Charlotte said. "You don't want to block the sign."

Bob cooperated and then turned off the engine as Charlotte opened the truck door to the late-afternoon heat.

"Char!" Bonnie Simons trotted down the front steps, her smile as bright as the red gladioli blooming in the front flowerbed.

Charlotte, with the bowl of salad in her hands, forced the pickup door shut with her hip. "Hello!" she called out, following Emily and Christopher toward the house.

"Where's Pete?" Bob came around from the driver's side.

"He's out back, grilling the steaks." Bonnie stretched out her arms for the salad. "It's so good to see you!" she said as Charlotte slipped the bowl into her hands. Bonnie seemed particularly animated today.

"I was surprised Pete and Dana were up to having all of us over." Charlotte walked with Bonnie up the stairs to the front door while Emily and Christopher followed their grandfather through the side gate.

"Well," Bonnie said, opening the screen door. She turned toward Charlotte as she passed through the doorway, her eyes sparkling. "They have—"

Dana, calling out from the kitchen, interrupted her. "There you are!" She rushed through the door, flinging a dishtowel over her shoulder. Next came Dana's grandmother,

Grandma Maxie, heading toward Charlotte with her arms outstretched for a hug. As they embraced, Charlotte wondered what in the world Bonnie Simons had been referring to before she was interrupted. Perhaps Dana and Pete did have a buyer for the house.

"Come on into the kitchen," Grandma Maxie said. "I'll pour you a glass of lemonade." Her gray hair was pulled back at the nape of her neck into her signature bun, and she wore a practical skirt and a red blouse. As always, her blue eyes sparkled.

Charlotte followed the older woman past Dana's piano; behind her, Bonnie and Dana walked side by side. "Hold on a sec," Charlotte overheard Bonnie say to Dana. "I need to ask you something."

Charlotte's heart constricted just a little at the conspiratorial tone, her thoughts landing for a second on her daughter, Denise, gone now for more than two years. She swung through the door into the kitchen.

"Sit down," Grandma Maxie said, pointing to a chair. She poured lemonade from a pitcher into a tall glass. "I always feel like I should be on a farm this time of year." She handed the glass to Charlotte. "Cooking for the men. Canning with my mother and grandmother—tomatoes, peaches, beans. Our pressure cooker worked overtime." She smiled.

"I need to put up more tomatoes," Charlotte said. As she spoke, the kitchen door swung open, and Bonnie came through, laugh lines dancing on her plump face. She pulled Dana behind her. "Let's all go outside," she said. "Pete and Dana have an announcement to make."

Dana smiled, her dark hair bobbing against her shoulders.

Charlotte's eyes widened. Bonnie's enthusiasm made it

sound as if this might be more than a celebrate-the-sale-of-a-house get-together. Charlotte stood and followed Grandma Maxie to the back door. Bonnie giggled behind her, and in a moment they all stood in the backyard with Bob, Emily, and Christopher staring at them.

"Where's Sam?" Pete asked, dangling the long grill fork in his hand.

"He hasn't gotten back from Grand Island yet," Emily answered. "He's on his way."

Pete shot Dana a look, and she stepped to his side, putting her arm around him.

"I think we should wait to make our announcement until Sam gets here." Pete was trying to whisper, but he never had been very successful at being quiet.

"I don't think Mom can wait," Dana replied in a normal tone.

Charlotte stole a glance at Bonnie. Hands clasped together, she stood beside her husband, Chuck, whose face held a look of confusion.

Christopher, who stood by the gate, began to wave his hand. "Sam just pulled up!"

"Whew." Pete tossed the fork into the air and barely caught it as it tumbled back to earth. "I'd hate to make this announcement twice."

Christopher opened the gate and yelled for Sam to hurry, Bob stepped closer to Charlotte, and Emily began peeling pink polish from her thumbnail.

"What's going on?" Sam hurried through the gate, his curly hair askew and the sleeves of his shirt pushed up to his elbows. It seemed to be his new college look.

Pete grinned and then put the fork on the picnic table. "Dana and I have some news."

Charlotte's heart began to race.

"Do you want to have the honors?" Pete asked Dana. She quickly shook her head.

Pete took a deep breath, looked around the gathering, and then said, "Dana's pregnant!" His arm shot up in the air, punctuating the two words.

Bonnie began clapping before Pete even finished. "I already knew!" Bonnie grabbed Charlotte's arm. "I guessed a couple of weeks ago. I couldn't wait for them to tell everyone."

A *baby!* How could she have been so dense? Charlotte put her arm out to hug Bonnie.

"I know this is old hat to you," Bonnie said, hugging Charlotte back. "But this is my first. I am so excited!" She held Charlotte tightly.

"Oh, no, it never gets to be old hat," Charlotte said, looking over Bonnie's shoulder. It was Pete's first baby, after all, and she couldn't be more excited—or more surprised. Bob was shaking Pete's hand, and Chuck had Dana in a bear hug. Christopher and Sam were high-fiving each other, but Emily stood back a little, her arms crossed.

Bonnie finally released Charlotte and headed toward Dana, pulling her away from Chuck and embracing her tightly. Maxie stepped beside Charlotte.

"You're going to be a great-grandmother," Charlotte said, taking the older woman's wrinkled hand.

"What a blessing," Grandma Maxie said, swiping at her eyes with the fingertips of her other hand. "And to think I'm still young enough to really enjoy it." She smiled through her tears.

It was true; Maxie was healthy and alert. She would probably even be able to help take care of the baby. Charlotte's thoughts drifted toward future great-grandchildren of her own as Sam yanked Christopher into a headlock. Sam would be nineteen in a few more months. Charlotte let out a little gasp. God willing, it would be years before he, or any of her other grandchildren, were parents.

Dana pulled away from her mom and smiled at Charlotte as she stepped forward, arms outstretched. "Congratulations," Charlotte said. "I couldn't be happier for you and Pete." She reveled in the blessing of her family, ever expanding.

"Pete, are those steaks almost done?" Bonnie asked, and then before he could answer, she turned toward her daughter again. "Dana, we should finish up the rest of the food."

Dana let go of Charlotte, and Bonnie wrapped her arm around Dana's waist. A wave of loss swept over Charlotte again. She had never had time with Denise and her babies the way Bonnie would have with Dana and this grandbaby. Bonnie, Dana, and Grandma Maxie headed up the steps to the kitchen.

Charlotte followed, wondering if the three women knew how truly blessed they were. She stopped on the top step and then turned and said, "Come on, Emily. You can help carry the food."

Emily flicked a piece of polish from her finger, wrinkled her nose, and then followed Charlotte into the house. Grandma Maxie asked Dana how she was feeling, and Dana explained that she'd had some morning sickness the first few weeks but was feeling better, although she had been tired since school started. "I went to bed at seven every night the first week of school," she said.

Bonnie asked Emily to squeeze more lemons, and when

Emily had a hard time using the juicer, Bonnie was surprised to learn the Stevensons didn't make their own lemonade. "You use the powdered stuff?" she asked, taking a step back.

"No. The frozen stuff," Emily answered, making a sour face.

Charlotte shot her granddaughter a *don't worry about it* look, plunked a spoon in the potato salad, and headed out to the backyard.

Hollyhocks grew along the fence, zinnias still bloomed in the corner flowerbed, and the grass was neatly edged. Charlotte seldom stopped by Pete and Dana's, and if she did, she never ventured out to the backyard.

"The steaks are done," Pete called out. Dana must have heard him in the house, because a second later the rest of the ladies, including Emily, paraded down the steps with the food.

A blue-checked tablecloth covered the picnic table, and they all gathered around it. Pete said a quick blessing, thanking the Lord for the food and the baby. Everyone smiled broadly as he said, "Amen," except for Emily, who was picking at her nail polish again. She stopped when Charlotte caught her eye.

"Do you have a name for the baby?" Christopher asked.

Pete shook his head. "We just call it *It* right now." He patted Dana's belly, and she pushed him away in fun.

Christopher scowled.

"We don't know if the baby is a boy or a girl," Dana said. "We'll have an ultrasound in a couple of months, so we'll have to decide by then whether we want to know ahead of time."

"Of course you'll want to know," Bonnie said.

"I'm pretty sure it's a boy," Christopher said before anyone could respond to Bonnie.

Sam threw his wadded-up napkin at Christopher. "How would you know?"

Christopher shrugged and shoved a potato chip into his mouth. "I thought Will was going to be a boy, and I was right about that," he said.

Charlotte shook her head at Christopher, reminding him not to talk with food in his mouth. She liked the idea of another baby boy in the family. Will, the son of her child, Bill, and his wife, Anna, would be just over a year older than Pete and Dana's baby. His sisters, Madison and Jennifer, had each other. It would be fun for Will to have a cousin to pal around with. It was amazing to think that Bill and Pete, who were ten years apart, would have children so close in age. Charlotte was sorry Bill and his family hadn't been able to join in the celebration tonight, but they would hear the news shortly.

"What do you think, Emily?" Bonnie asked. "Should Dana and Pete find out if it's a boy or a girl?"

Emily shrugged as she pushed a chunk of watermelon around her plate. "It's their call." Charlotte searched her granddaughter's face, but Emily wasn't giving anything away.

AS EMILY CLEARED THE TABLE, picking up the near-empty bag of chips, her cell phone vibrated in the pocket of her jeans. She reflexively dug it out and checked the number. It wasn't one she recognized. Maybe it was Troy, calling from a landline.

"Hello, this is Emily," she said in her sweetest voice.

"Hey, it's Isabella." Isabella Dobbs had been trying to attach herself to Emily and Ashley since the first day of school two weeks ago.

"Oh, hi." Emily tucked the phone between her head and shoulder and rolled the bag of chips closed. "What's up?"

"I need the English assignment. I forgot it at school."

"It's at home—I can call you later."

"Where are you?"

"My aunt and uncle's." Emily walked to the other side of the picnic table, not wanting anyone to overhear her conversation.

"Mrs. Stevenson's?" Isabella's voice had that dramatic tone to it.

"Yes." Emily's voice dropped.

"Just ask her, silly."

Emily stepped to where she could look into the house through the back door. Dana—Mrs. Stevenson—was putting chunks of watermelon into a container. "Um, no. But I'll call you when I get home."

"Oh, never mind," Isabella said. "I'll call Ashley." The two said good-bye, and Emily hit END on her phone and wiggled it back into her pocket. That was weird. What was even weirder was that Aunt Dana was her English teacher this year, which everyone knew and teased her about.

Well, not exactly everyone. Isabella was the main one—she was turning into a real gossip. She couldn't seem to stop talking about Emily being Mrs. Stevenson's niece, and she was always commenting about Emily getting special treatment, which wasn't true at all. If anything, Aunt Dana expected more from Emily and was always calling on her when no one else knew the answer. The only bright spot was that Troy was a senior, which meant he wasn't in the class, so she didn't have to be humiliated in front of him nearly every day.

"Want to shoot hoops?" Christopher stood with a basketball in his hands in front of the gate to the side yard, which was wide open.

"We're probably going home soon," Emily said.

"Probably not." Christopher tried to spin the ball on his index finger, but it tumbled to the grass.

Maybe Sam would take her home. "I'll be out in a minute." She headed into the kitchen.

"And Emily—" Bonnie turned toward her as she came through the door. "You can babysit!"

Emily had recently babysat for Will and had had quite a scare when he choked on a grape. She hoped she'd feel confident enough to babysit a newborn. Emily loved Will, but for some reason she had a weird feeling about Dana's news. "So, like..." Emily turned toward Dana. "Are you going to, you know..."

"Come on, use your English." Bonnie laughed as if she'd told the funniest joke ever.

Emily scowled.

"What is it, Em?" Dana asked, stepping closer.

"Are you going to tell people at school?"

"Well, I haven't told anyone yet. What do you think? Should I tell everyone right away?" She smiled.

"I don't know." Emily wedged the bag of chips between the lemonade pitcher and the empty watermelon bowl. It wasn't that she cared when Aunt Dana told people; she just wanted to know ahead of time before everyone in English class started talking about it. Ashley would be really excited, but some of the other kids might make comments —and Isabella would definitely be weird about it.

"I'll probably wait a few more weeks, until I'm through my first trimester. Unless you want everyone to know sooner." Dana's dimples flashed.

Emily shook her head. "No, that's fine. Whatever you decide is cool." She sighed. "I'm going outside—to shoot hoops." *And ask Sam for a ride home.*

BACK AT HEATHER CREEK FARM, Charlotte stood in the middle of the back lawn, between the barn and the house, and watched the full moon ease past a wisp of cloud covering its bottom half. The warm, muggy night felt heavy as she took a shallow breath.

Toby nuzzled her hand, and Charlotte rubbed the dog's head. "How are you, girl?" she cooed. Toby stepped closer, her tail batting against Charlotte's leg.

The screen door squeaked. "Char?" Bob stepped out under the porch light.

"I'll be there in a minute." She stopped rubbing Toby's head, and the dog settled on the ground beside her.

"No hurry." In a moment he stood beside her. "Pretty moon," he said.

She nodded. It was the harvest moon, sailing low and bright.

Bob crossed his arms, looping his thumbs around his suspenders. "I don't know what Pete's thinking, having a baby so soon."

"Pardon?" Charlotte searched her husband's face to see if he was serious. There was no hint of a smile. "We were much, much younger when I got pregnant with Bill."

"That was different." Bob's voice was gruff.

Charlotte suppressed a laugh, and Toby hopped to her feet.

"We had a house, and I was running the farm. He's building one house and trying to sell another, and he hasn't taken over the farm yet. And he hasn't proven himself ready for that either."

"Sweetie, he's thirty-four."

"My point exactly," Bob said, rubbing his chin.

Charlotte took a deep breath. "You were running the farm because your dad turned it over to you completely."

"Because he could trust me to make enough money to support all of us."

"And when are you planning to turn the farm over to Pete?" Charlotte asked gently.

Bob crossed his arms. "I had been thinking maybe I would do it sometime soon—but now I'm not so sure. Let's see how he handles things through the rest of harvest. And how things work out with his house." Bob narrowed his eyes. "And the bank loan he negotiated. All of that."

Charlotte kept quiet. Pete had a tall order ahead of him.

"I'm going inside."

"Give me another minute," Charlotte said.

Bob stumbled a little as he reached the walkway but regained his balance and lumbered on to the back door. When was he going to forgive Pete for acting like an adolescent all those years ago? Charlotte sighed and tipped her head back. She wasn't going to think about Bob, the farm, and Pete. There were more important things to focus on right now. This baby would be her seventh grandchild. She shivered happily regardless of the warm night. God was good.

Chapter Two

"Grandma, why can't I take your car?" Emily sidled up to the kitchen counter, her green-gray eyes wide. "I'm a good driver, honest."

"Honey, we're not going to have you driving to school." Charlotte thought she'd already been clear about the subject. "You can use the car to go to youth group, that sort of thing. Or run errands."

"I thought you said I could drive to school." Emily's voice was shrill.

"No, I never said that." Charlotte knew she needed to defuse the conversation. She touched Emily's shoulder. "I'm sorry if I was unclear before, but now you know. We need to move on from this."

"Let's go." Christopher stood at the back door with his backpack in his hand. "Or we're going to miss the bus."

Emily stomped away from the counter, grabbed her backpack off the table, and followed Christopher out the door. Charlotte dried her hands on a towel and decided to walk the children to the bus.

"I'm the only junior in the entire county who takes the bus," Emily said, kicking at a rock as they reached the driveway. "Probably the entire state. It's torture."

Charlotte knew that wasn't true but didn't say anything. Charlotte needed her car during the day, and the family couldn't afford to finance another car for Emily to drive.

"Why can't I drive, Grandma? Don't you trust me?"

"Of course I trust you. I need my car—that's all." She paused. "Will you be seeing Troy this week?" she asked, trying to change the subject.

Emily shrugged. "I don't know." The two had been dating since last spring. "He's been working a lot lately."

Charlotte was hoping that was the case. He washed dishes for a steak house in Harding, and as far as she was concerned, even though he was a nice boy, the busier he was the better. Hopefully he was saving his money to go to college next year—but chances were that most of it was going for gas for his truck.

Emily increased her stride. "You're not going to walk us all the way to the bus stop are you?" she asked, looking over her shoulder.

"That's my plan."

Emily winced.

"Hurry!" Christopher had reached the road. "The bus is almost here."

"Bye!" Emily called out, waving at Charlotte as she started to run.

"Have a good day." Charlotte stopped. "See you after school."

Emily reached the road just as the bus came to a stop. Christopher bent down, petted Toby good-bye, and then started up the steps.

"Come on, girl," Charlotte called out to the dog, and Toby spun around, darting back up the lane, barking at a squirrel that scurried among the elm trees that made up the windbreak. It was a beautiful morning with a gorgeous blue sky, not a cloud in sight. The mugginess from the night before had vanished with the thunderstorm that woke her just past midnight. It had been the third storm in a week.

Toby stopped and sniffed a stick in the grass alongside the driveway and then picked it up in her mouth. She turned toward Charlotte.

Charlotte took the stick from Toby and then extended her arm, hurling it up in the air. It twirled toward the barn. She still had a good throw left in her, old grandma that she was. "Go get it, girl!"

Bob headed across the lawn with his coffee cup in his hand. "Where's Pete?" he called out.

Charlotte had hoped a good night's sleep would cure Bob of his negativity. She sighed.

"He should have been here an hour or more ago." Bob was right; Pete should have been here by now, but he wasn't.

"Something must have come up," Charlotte said.

"Like what? Sleeping in?"

Toby returned with the stick, and Charlotte threw it again, this time an easy underhand lob. It had been years since Pete was prone to sleeping in, but the memory was seared in Bob's mind, and she could hardly blame him for still remembering. Pete would promise he was going to take farming seriously, and then he would oversleep day after day. Bob would trudge up the stairs to Pete's apartment over the shed, which only made Pete angry. Finally Charlotte convinced Bob not to wake him. After he slept in until noon two days in a row, Bob placed an ad in the *Bedford Leader* for a farmhand. Pete saw it the next day and hadn't overslept since.

"He'll be here," Charlotte said, taking the stick from Toby again. This time her aim wasn't so good. She accidentally lobbed it toward the garden, and it bounced into Christopher's pumpkin patch. She hurried after the dog. She didn't want Toby digging in the plants.

As she reached the garden, she heard the sound of a vehicle's tires rolling over the gravel and turned, expecting to see Pete's old Ford pickup rounding the turn. Instead it was Frank Carter in his old Chevy. It was hard to believe it had been just three months since his bypass surgery. He wasn't back to working full-time, but he was definitely getting around.

She dug the stick out from between the gigantic leaves and threw it into the pasture, brushed her hands, and walked back toward Bob. It hadn't entered her head that maybe Pete had had an accident on the way out to the farm—but now she felt a measure of concern creep up her spine, wondering if their neighbor had brought bad news.

"What's Frank up to?" Bob raised his mug to his mouth and took a swallow.

Frank parked by Charlotte's car and then climbed from his truck, tipping his straw hat as he did. "Howdy," he called out, twirling a leaf in his hand. He didn't seem upset.

"What brings you out so early?" Bob wrapped both of his hands around the coffee cup.

"I have a question for Pete." Frank glanced around. "Is he out in the field?"

"Actually...," Charlotte said, just as she registered the sound of a second vehicle.

"Well, well," Bob said, turning. "Look who decided to show up for work after all."

Pete was driving fast, and pieces of gravel spurted out

from under his tires as his old green pickup careened around the curve. Toby began barking, running along behind the truck.

"Where's the fire?" Frank asked and then laughed. Charlotte attempted a smile at Frank's reference to Pete's years as a volunteer fireman as her son parked by the shed and jumped to the ground.

"Is everything okay?" Charlotte asked, shading her eyes from the morning sun.

"I hope so." He grabbed his baseball cap and yanked it over his uncombed hair. "Dana was up most of the night."

"Is she sick?"

"Or ate something that didn't agree with her." He walked toward them. "I fixed her some tea and toast and then cleaned up."

Bob crossed his arms. Pete ignored his dad and headed toward Frank.

"Good morning." Pete shook their old friend's hand firmly. "What have you got there?" Pete nodded at the leaf.

"Well." Frank held up his hand. "I wondered if you've noticed any spots on your soybean plants."

"Spots?" Pete took the leaf.

"It looks like a fungus. I noticed a few the day before yesterday and then a few more this morning when I was walking through the field."

"It's late in the season for a fungus," Bob said, handing Charlotte his cup and then taking the leaf from Pete. He pulled his reading glasses from his pocket.

"I don't know what else it would be," Frank said.

"Our crop looks good." Pete rubbed his hands together. "I'm counting on it to pay off our loan."

Charlotte inhaled. She did not want to discuss their latest

loan in front of Frank; she was sure that he and Hannah were able to operate their farm without credit. Of course, they weren't supporting two families either.

Frank took the leaf back. "Well, let me know if you find anything."

"We'll go check right now," Bob said.

"I said we didn't have any." Pete shoved his hands into the pockets of his jeans.

"Let's go," Bob said to Pete, marching toward his truck. Pete followed, looking like a chastised puppy.

"Tell Hannah hello," Charlotte called after Frank as he climbed into his truck.

The two pickups pulled out, one by one, and headed down the drive with Bob in the lead. "Well," Charlotte said to Toby, holding Bob's still-warm coffee cup in her hands, "there they go."

Fifteen minutes later, Charlotte shook the dirt from the roots of a weed as she worked between the tomato plants and the green bean vines in the garden. The morning sun warmed her back as she made her way up the row. The garden had already peaked and was just beginning to wither even though the temperature hadn't dropped anywhere near the freezing level, and she was still watering daily. She hoped to harvest as much as possible in the few weeks that remained. When she reached the end of the row, she straightened her back, stretching for a moment, as Bob's truck rolled back up the driveway, this time much slower.

Pete and Bob climbed from the cab, and Charlotte stepped out of the garden, the hint of a smile starting to spread across her face as she slipped her gardening gloves from her hands. But then she realized Pete held a bunch of leaves in his hand. Charlotte started across the lawn. "Do our plants have it too?" she called out, increasing her pace.

"Just a few," Pete said.

"He missed them." Bob squinted at her, the lines around his eyes heavy.

"Dad, there weren't any before. I would have noticed."

"I don't know—you've had your mind on other things."

Pete increased his stride. "I'm going to go call Frank and then call around to the other neighbors."

"I can go tell Frank." Charlotte tucked her gloves under her arm. "I have a cake pan that I need to return to Hannah."

"Thanks." Pete extended half the leaves to her. "Take these along—have Frank compare them to his. I'll take the rest to the extension office."

Charlotte nodded. She hated to have him miss the work time to go into Harding, but a possible fungus needed to be addressed immediately. "Bob, want to come along?"

"Sure," he said. "I'll drive."

THEY PULLED INTO Frank and Hannah's driveway a few minutes later, making their way down the dirt road between the lush green soybean plants on one side and the golden head-high corn on the other.

Frank came out of his shed, surprised to see them. Bob held up the handful of leaves after he parked the truck. He opened the door and called out, "Pete was wrong. We've got it too."

"Come on in for some coffee," Frank said. "Hannah just started a fresh pot."

The Carters' two-story house was surrounded by shade trees—maple, oak, and birch. Charlotte reached the back door first, knocked, called out, "Yoo-hoo, Hannah," and entered.

A few minutes later the four of them sat around Hannah's kitchen table, drinking coffee and enjoying her lemon bars.

"Maybe it's one of those strains that's resistant to fungicide," Frank said, looking at the pile of leaves and a few browning seed pods spread between them.

"Could be," Bob said.

"Well, it doesn't sound like the crop is covered or anything. We're so close to harvest that maybe it won't make that much difference." Hannah folded her napkin and then ran it across the powdered sugar that had fallen on the table.

"That's right," Frank said. "There's no reason not to be optimistic."

Bob wiped his mouth with the back of his hand.

"Pete is taking a sample to the extension agent," Charlotte said. "Maybe he'll have more information." She was afraid Frank and Hannah's optimism was closer to denial.

"It's not like this is rocket science," Bob said and then drained his coffee cup. "There has to be an answer."

WHEN BOB AND CHARLOTTE arrived home, there was a list on the dining room table with the last names of nearby neighbors. The Carters' name had a checkmark next to it, but none by the rest of the names, including the Freemans, Barrys, Maynards, and Driggers. Pete had probably ended up leaving messages for everyone. That meant that Charlotte would most likely be taking messages, starting around noon, for the rest of the day.

Sure enough, just as she and Bob sat down for a lunch of leftover meatloaf, green salad, and baked sweet potatoes the phone rang. It was Dick Barry, whose property was adjacent to Heather Creek Farm. He got right down to business. "Got Pete's message. Tell him we don't have any spots, but I thank him for asking." Charlotte could hardly get in, "Thank you for calling back," before Dick was saying his good-byes.

"Tell Eulalia hello," Charlotte said as Dick hung up.

She took a second to write no beside his name on the list.

Charlotte sat back down at the table, and Bob said a blessing over the food, but just as he said, "Amen," the phone rang again.

"I'm going to let the machine get that," Charlotte said.

"Good idea." Bob passed her the salad. "There's no reason for you to be Pete's answering service."

As they ate, they listened to the muffled voice over the machine. "It's Silas Maynard. We don't have no fungus." He hung up without saying good-bye.

Bob gave Charlotte a bemused look. A couple of minutes later, as Bob talked about the tractor repairs he was making, the phone rang again. Soon Walt Freeman's voice was floating into the dining room, but Bob raised his volume and they both tuned out Walt.

IT WAS FIVE AFTER SIX when Pete listened to the last voice mail. "It's only us and the Carters." He sat at the dining room table with the phone in his hand.

"What did you find out in Harding?" Charlotte spooned green beans into a serving dish.

Pete leaned back in his chair. "The extension office was closed. Tim Olson was out in the field."

"Oh, that's too bad." Not only had he taken a chunk of time off but it had also been wasted. "Frank thought maybe it's fungicide resistant," Charlotte said.

"That could be." Pete took a deep breath. "All I know is we need this crop. And we need our house to sell." He rubbed the back of his neck.

"You all right?"

"Fine. Just tired."

"You should get on home to Dana."

Pete was on his feet in a second. "Yep. You're right. I'm out of here." He waved and then sauntered out the door.

"Is Uncle Pete okay?" It was Emily, her voice quiet as she stood in the doorway to the hall.

"He's fine," Charlotte said. "You know, it's been one of those days."

"Da—I mean Aunt Dana—was late for school today."

"She was sick last night." Charlotte picked up the bowl of beans, breathing in the fresh aroma.

"Because of the baby?" Emily followed Charlotte toward the table.

"Oh, I don't think so," Charlotte said. "Pete thought it might have been something she ate. Go call your brothers for dinner, okay? And Grandpa too. I think he's asleep in his chair."

THAT EVENING Emily sat at her desk, staring at the stack of magazines in front of her. Her assignment for English was to make a "Who Am I?" collage about herself and what she wanted out of life. It seemed like one of those assignments that Aunt Dana came up with at the last minute because she didn't want to correct papers tomorrow night.

It was the kind of assignment that Emily usually loved. She twirled her favorite paper scissors on her finger, spinning them off in a clatter onto her desk. She picked up her glue stick and took off the cap. The glue was purple; she smeared a little on the paper and watched the color disappear.

She used to make collages a lot back in California. She would watch TV after school and cut and paste. She would make cards cutting out letters to spell "Happy Birthday" or "Merry Christmas" or whatever the occasion was. She mostly made cards for her mom.

She tapped her foot under her desk and flipped through the magazine, stopping at a photo spread of spring fashions. The shoot had taken place in New York City's Central Park. She began clipping a photo of a model wearing a black-and-white A-line dress while standing next to a horse-drawn carriage. She did like horses so that showed a little of herself as well.

"Emily?" Grandma was knocking. "Are you almost done with your homework?" She eased the door open.

"Just about." She'd already done her history and chemistry assignments. "I saved the easiest for last."

Grandma, wearing her old ratty robe and slippers, stepped toward her. "What are you working on?"

"A collage for English."

"Oh?" Grandma was looking over her shoulder now.

"It's supposed to show who we are and where we're going."

"Nice," Grandma said. "What ideas do you have for who you are?"

"Oh, I was going to include a photo of me. I have some leftover school pictures from last year."

"That's a good idea. Are you going to show your family too?"

Emily turned toward Grandma and wrinkled her nose. "You mean put photos of Sam and Christopher on my collage?"

"Sure," Grandma said. "You are a sister—and a granddaughter and a niece." She smiled.

Emily looked at her collage again. *A niece.* Did that mean she should include a photo of Pete and Dana? That would be weird. A random thought crept into her head—Grandma and Dana at school conferences this year. She started to smile and then stopped, wondering what Dana would say to Grandma.

"Well, don't stay up too late." Grandma patted Emily's shoulder. "Get a good rest."

"You too," Emily said, her eyes still on her collage. "See you in the morning."

After a moment she put down her scissors and pushed her chair back. Who was she? Someone who liked to design clothes and sew sometimes. Someone who wanted out of Bedford.

Grandma was right. She was a sister and those other things too. Was she still a daughter, even though she no longer had a mother? She did have a father; she just didn't have much of a relationship with him. Her eyes began to water. Maybe this wasn't such a great assignment after all, not for her anyway. It was a good one for Ashley, though, with her normal family.

It wasn't like all the other kids didn't already know Emily's story—but that didn't mean she wanted to rehash the whole thing again.

She stood and walked to the window, pushing back the curtain and swiping at her eyes. In the distance, lightning flashed across the dark sky. Toby was probably shaking in her doghouse—maybe she'd come inside and sleep with Christopher.

They were supposed to be reading *To Kill a Mockingbird* for English class. Sam said he'd had to read it two years ago too. Isabella had asked Miss Simons—make that Mrs. Stevenson, or Aunt Dana—why they had to read a book written about race issues in the South during the 1930s. Aunt Dana had said the novel was a classic and dealt with universal issues.

Another streak of lightning flashed across the sky. Emily counted slowly. *One, two, three, four, five, six, sev—*. The thunder sounded faint. The storm was still far away.

She mostly found herself not calling her new aunt anything in class, afraid she was going to call her the wrong thing. *Miss Simons. Dana. Mrs. Stevenson. Aunt Dana.* Too many names. She felt for kids who had a parent as a teacher. That would be even worse.

A few minutes later another flash filled the sky followed by an immediate crash of thunder; before the clatter stopped her door flew open, and Christopher came stumbling into her room. "That was right on top of us!" he yelled.

Emily stepped closer to the window, expecting the oak tree to be split in two, but she couldn't see anything in the darkness until another flash lit up the sky. But then all she could make out was the yard and the field beyond it, eerily illuminated by the electrical display. Again the crash was instantaneous.

"Get away from the window!" Christopher yelled.

Emily stepped into the middle of the room as Christopher dove under her quilt on the bed.

"It's okay." She sat on the bed and wrapped her arm around him.

"What if it hits the house?"

"There's a lightning rod on the roof."

"What if the house catches on fire?"

Emily climbed off the bed, snatching her phone off her desk as she spoke. "We'll climb out the window. I'll call 9-1-1."

Another crash of thunder shook the room, but it wasn't as loud.

"It's passing," Emily said, her arm around him again, her hand clenching her cell phone. It was funny to be comforting Christopher when he was nearly as tall as she was. But he was still her little brother. Sometimes it felt as if he would always be a little boy.

Another crash reverberated through the room but sounded farther in the distance. The curtain stirred as a breeze swelled through the open window, followed by the patter of rain. Christopher followed Emily to the window. The fresh scent of the storm mixed with the ripening fields and the freshly plowed soil across the road and filled Emily's lungs as she breathed in deeply.

"I'm glad that's over," Christopher said.

"But it was pretty exciting." Emily liked the thunderstorms that tore across the landscape; compared with a tornado they were pretty calm but still a thrill.

"I'd already had enough excitement for one day," Christopher said. He hadn't said anything after school or at dinner.

"Oh yeah?"

"Remember Justin Taylor?"

Emily nodded, closing the window against the rain now falling on the sill. "That kid who used to pick on you?"

"Used to?"

She sat back down on the bed. "What? Has he been at it again?"

Christopher nodded. "And he's going to start riding our bus. He said his family is renting a house past ours."

"Really?" Emily couldn't think of a place that would be for rent. "Where?"

"I don't know."

"Maybe he was messing with you, just trying to make you mad."

"Maybe."

"Hopefully." She tousled his strawlike hair just as her phone started to vibrate in her other hand. She checked the screen. It was Troy.

"Hey," she said to Christopher, holding up her cell. "The storm's over. You need to get into bed."

Christopher nodded, stood, and shuffled toward the door as Emily said hello.

"I'm on my way home," he said. "What are you up to?"

She told him about her English project.

"We did that last year."

"Oh." Emily had been sure it was a spur-of-the-moment assignment.

"Yeah. It's supposed to build empathy or something."

He paused and then said, "I can't remember how, but it's somehow related to *To Kill a Mockingbird*."

Emily wrinkled her nose. That seemed like a stretch. "You work tomorrow, right?"

"Yep. And the next day and the next."

She sighed. "Guess I'll see you at school."

"Guess so," he answered.

As they said good-bye, Emily's phone beeped with another incoming call, but she ignored it. A moment later she checked the number: it was the one Isabella had called from the night before.

Not wanting to call Isabella back—she'd probably forgotten the assignment again—Emily tried to refocus on the collage. She was Troy's girlfriend, but she certainly wasn't going to put that on the collage. She pressed the glue stick against a piece of scrap paper and held it up, yawned, and then checked her cell. *9:30*. It wasn't too late to call Ashley.

It took her friend four long rings to answer. "Hi, Em." She spoke quickly. "I have Isabella on the other line so I can't chat, but listen to this: she thinks her parents are going to make an offer on Pete and Dana's house. Isn't that cool?"

"Sure." Emily knew it was good news for Pete and Dana but not for her. Isabella would make some sort of drama out of all of it.

"Okay, gotta go," Ashley said. "Mom said no more calls tonight. See you tomorrow."

Emily said good-bye, pushed END, and stepped back to the window, suddenly overcome by loneliness.

Chapter Three

Pete opened his pickup door, started to climb in, and then turned around abruptly. He'd better let Mom know he was headed to Harding. He didn't want Dad to come to the conclusion he was skipping out early on a Friday. He had meant to make it back to Harding on Thursday, but he'd lost track of time, and when he finally remembered, he realized the extension office would be closed.

"Mom?" He stood at the edge of the kitchen linoleum, aware of his muddy boots. "Mom!" he called out again.

"In here." It sounded like she was in the family room.

He heard the creak of a chair as he stepped across the kitchen. "I'm headed to the extension office."

She appeared with her embroidery in her hand. "I'm glad you stopped before you went in. Silas called a few minutes ago. He found some spots on his soybean plants."

"Really?" Pete rubbed the back of his neck. "So that's three of us—all with property along the creek." The Maynard farm was a small place directly across from the Carters'.

Charlotte nodded.

"But no one else has spots?"

She nodded again.

"Okay—I'll be back shortly." He smiled. "Just keep Dad off my back, okay?"

"Pete." She gave him that disapproving look.

"Just kidding." He waved as he hustled toward the door.

Forty-five minutes later he stood in the extension office, rubbing the back of his head. Tim Olson held the clump of leaves in his hands. "You have even more today?"

Pete nodded.

"It definitely looks like a fungus. Are you sure you sprayed a fungicide?"

"Yep." There had been some confusion with the spraying last spring, but that had been in one part of the field.

"Positive?" Tim had a little bit of a smirk on his face. Pete had thought that story hadn't gotten around, but now he wasn't so sure. "It's late in the season for a fungus."

"We know," Pete said. He'd said that when he'd first come through the door. "So you haven't had anyone else reporting a fungus like this?"

"No." Tim pushed the leaves back across the counter. "Do you have any enemies? Maybe someone sprayed your plants in the dead of night." He chuckled.

Pete didn't think it was funny. "Frank Carter's and Silas Maynard's crops have spots too."

"That right?" Tim stroked his goatee. "You might check with the ag department at Harding College."

"Sounds like a good idea." Pete scooped up the leaves and headed out the door.

EMILY COULDN'T TAKE HER EYES off Isabella as she stood at the front of the classroom, her collage in her hand.

Her dark hair hung down to her shoulders, and her ultra-short bangs were sticking up in five different directions. She wore a black vest over a red blouse, cargo pants, and thick-soled black shoes. She wasn't large, but the baggy clothes made her appear bigger than she was. She swung her poster board around as she waited for everyone in the class to focus on her.

"Go ahead," Dana said.

Isabella's collage was divided into two sections: *Now* and *Later.* Everyone laughed as she read her title, and she joined in. "I get it," she said. "Now and Later—I didn't mean it like the candy though." She smiled widely.

"Okay," Isabella continued. "Now I live in Bedford, Nebraska. I am a student. And a singer." She had a map of Nebraska with Bedford circled and a photo of the choir from last year. She had cut out the letters S-I-N-G-E-R from a magazine. She did like to sing; choir was her favorite class. "I hope to someday go to Nashville—*later*." She smiled as a few kids laughed.

"But first I'll go to college and take music theory, maybe at Princeton or Yale." Everyone laughed again. Everyone knew her grades weren't that good. "Or Central Community College in Grand Island."

She shrugged. Her collage had pictures of a keyboard, a guitar, and a cityscape, presumably Nashville. "That's it," she said, grinning and then bobbing her poster board up and down as she marched back to her seat.

Dana, who was leaning against her desk, clapped and then asked Ashley to present her project. Ashley practically skipped to the front of the classroom, holding her collage. Her red hair was up on her head, and she wore a purple blouse with a thin gold scarf around her neck. She looked gorgeous.

Isabella leaned forward as Ashley began to talk. The first photo she explained was a picture of her as a little girl; she was supercute with red ringlets and rosy cheeks. Then she pointed to a photo taken just last year of her family right after her mom beat cancer. They all looked so happy sitting on their sofa, smiling at the camera. She had the words *sister*, *daughter*, and *cancer hater* on her collage.

Ashley pointed to her second section. "As far as where I'm headed . . ." She touched a cutout of a Race for the Cure ad. "I want to be involved in research to find a way to defeat cancer. So I plan to go to college—I'm not sure where—and study biomedicine." She smiled. "Plus, I want to be a mom someday."

There was a photo from a magazine of a cute redheaded little boy. "And I would like to live on a farm." She pointed to a magazine photo of a big, old rambling house in the middle of a field. "And I would like to travel." She'd pasted magazine photos of an airplane, train, and ship.

"Thank—" Dana started to say.

"I'm not quite done." Ashley smiled sweetly as she turned her collage over. On the back was the word *Jeremiah* and the numbers *29* and *11*.

"This is my life verse. I found it when my mom had cancer. I picked up my Bible one night, and this is where it fell open. It's both who I am and where I'm going." She quoted it out loud: "'For I know the plans I have for you,' declares the LORD, 'plans to prosper you and not to harm you, plans to give you hope and a future.'"

Ashley looked radiant as Dana began to clap. "That was lovely, Ashley, just lovely."

Isabella turned toward Emily. "That's so cool," she whispered.

Emily nodded. She vaguely remembered hearing that verse at church. It was poetic, and it made her shiver. God had never given her a verse, not even when her mother died. Not that she'd been reading her Bible back then—or much now, really. She couldn't imagine anyone in San Diego including a Bible verse on her Who Am I? collage.

"Emily?" Had Aunt Dana been talking to her long? "Are you ready?"

"Yes." But she wasn't; she didn't want to follow Ashley. She shuffled to the front of the classroom with her collage in her hand.

"Who am I?" She pointed to the photo of Britney in the corral. "I love horses." Her friend Hunter smiled as she spoke. "And designing and sewing." She moved her finger next to the photo of her in the prom dress she had designed, and then on to a photo of her and Ashley during her fifteenth birthday party at the bowling alley. They were hamming it up with the bowling balls posed under their chins. "And I'm a good friend." She was aware of both Aunt Dana and Ashley nodding.

"As far as where I'm going—"

"Wait!" Isabella waved her hand.

Emily blushed.

"What about your family?"

Emily shrugged, wanting to say that Isabella hadn't included *her* family.

"What about your aunt?" Isabella pointed at Dana, her purple nails looking like bruises on the ends of her fingers.

A look of discomfort settled on Aunt Dana's face.

"Plus you have brothers—"

But no mother. Or father—or not much of one. Emily shot Aunt Dana a desperate look.

Dana cleared her throat. "Isabella," she said, "let Emily continue please."

Isabella frowned and slumped against the back of her chair.

Emily took a deep breath. "Where am I going? Away from here," she said, pointing at the magazine photo taken in Central Park.

PETE SLOWED AS HE drove past the John Deere store on his way to the college, eyeing the luxury-model tractor he had wanted to buy last spring.

The corporate farm on the highway between Heather Creek Farm and Bedford had a tractor just like it. Funny how some people, even in a poor economy, could afford such extravagances. Well, he was done dreaming about new tractors because he had something much better headed his way. He sat up straighter on the pickup's bench seat patched with duct tape. He was going to be a father.

Boy, if someone had told him in high school when Dana broke up with him that someday they would get married and make a baby—well, he wouldn't have believed them; that was for sure. He turned onto the tree-lined residential street leading to the college and turned up the radio. Rodney Atkins sang "Watching You." Pete used to think the song about a boy looking up to his dad was corny, but now, as he hummed along, his eyes grew teary.

Pete swiped at his eyes and muttered, "Whoa. I better get

a grip." But he turned the song up even louder. The night before, he and Dana had talked about what they were going to do for child care when the baby came. She would be able to take off the rest of the year when the baby was born in the spring, and of course she'd be off in the summer, but then she would need to go back to work next fall.

The baby would be five months old then. He'd told her he could take the baby to work with him—put a car seat in his pickup and move it to the tractor. Maybe he and Dad could rig something up. When he walked the field he could put it in one of those baby packs.

Dana had started to smile as he talked. By the time he stopped she was laughing out loud, even though she didn't feel well.

"What?" he'd asked.

She just shook her head. "You'll see."

He passed the sign welcoming him to Harding College and then slowed for the first speed bump. He found a parking place under an elm tree, grabbed the pile of leaves, now wilted, and headed into the brick agriculture building and then down the stairs to the lab, pushing open the door.

Someone must have been working or it wouldn't have been unlocked, but he couldn't see anyone. "Howdy," he called out, but no one answered.

"Hey." He peered around the counter. Maybe they were next door in the department office. He pushed back through the office door and almost bumped into a woman in a lab coat.

"Excuse me," she said, darting sideways to avoid a collision. She looked to be in her forties and had short brown hair.

"I'm looking for someone in the lab. I have a question."

"I'm Dr. Anderson. I can help you." She motioned for him to follow her. "What do you have?"

"A mysterious fungus, I think." Pete spread the samples on the counter as she took her place on the other side.

"On wilted leaves." Her blue eyes twinkled as she smiled. "It's a little late in the season for a fungus."

Pete groaned. "That's what everyone says."

"How prevalent is it?"

"I have it in two fields—and two of my neighbors have it in theirs. It's not dense, but it's making itself known, mostly around the perimeter," he said.

She picked up a leaf and held it close. "What percentage of your crop is affected at this point?"

"I'd say 10 percent, maybe. And it's spreading."

"And when do you anticipate to start harvesting?"

"Three weeks. Or so."

She stood up straight. "It certainly looks like a fungus. I'll run some tests and get back to you." She slid a form and a pen toward Pete.

"Do you have any suggestions in the meantime?"

"You can pluck off the affected leaves."

"Seriously?"

She smiled. "That's what would have been done in the old days."

"And if I don't do anything?" Pete said as he bent over the form, filling in his name and phone number.

"It could continue to spread. Or not." She put a sample of the leaves into a plastic envelope and dangled it in midair. "I'll call early next week."

Pete extended his hand and shook hers. "Thank you."

ON HIS WAY BACK to the farm Pete decided to stop by the corporate farm. He hadn't called the other day to see if they had the fungus, but now he decided it was important information to have. If they did have it, maybe they'd already come up with a protocol to combat it. Maybe he and his band of family farmers could piggyback—for once—on the corporate farm's resources.

He turned into the lane, passing through the open gate, and by the carved wooden sign that read BRASK FARMS. Pete had lost track of how many acres were owned by the corporation, whose headquarters were in Chicago. Maybe five thousand by now. It wasn't huge compared to some places. But for Nebraska, a state that had an anti-farm-corporation law until just a few years ago, it was big.

Pastureland lined the lane, and in the far distance a sea of corn swayed in the breeze. In the field past the shop, the coveted John Deere tractor plowed the ground. Pete parked his truck and climbed out, squinting. If he were the foreman, he'd be on that tractor, but chances were, one of the hired men was driving it.

He walked around the shop on a thick layer of gravel, swiping the sleeve of his work shirt over his sweaty forehead. He came to a sign on a window that read OFFICE and then opened the door and stepped inside, calling out, "Howdy."

A voice from the rear of the shop called out, "Back here."

Pete walked between two desks with new computers and through an open door into a brightly lit room with two high tables.

"Be right with you," said a man, looking into a microscope. There were posters on one wall showing plants and leaves and microorganisms, and on the other wall was a chart of the periodic table.

The man jotted something down in the notebook beside the microscope and then looked up. "How can I help you?"

He appeared to be around forty, although he was as thin as a twenty-year-old. He wore jeans and a green T-shirt with the logo of the farm on the pocket.

Pete introduced himself as the man peeled off his latex gloves and then stepped around the end of the table to shake Pete's hand. "Slim Stanton," he said. "I'm the foreman here."

The man leaned against the table as Pete explained why he'd stopped by.

"A fungus? This late in the season?" The man stood up straight and crossed his arms.

Pete nodded. "I'm ninety-nine percent sure, but the lab in Harding is running tests." Pete gestured toward Slim's microscope. "Looks like you could probably do some tests yourself."

Slim shook his head. "Nah, I just check nitrate levels and that sort of thing. But I'll definitely let you know if it shows up here. We have three thousand acres of soy beans—I don't want to take any chances." Slim took a step toward the door, and Pete followed.

"Tell me again—where's your place?" Slim entered the office.

Pete hadn't told him before. "Heather Creek Farm, up the road."

"Oh, I know exactly where it is. It's a really nice place—just beautiful." He opened the front door.

"It's been in the family for over a hundred years," Pete said as he stepped out into the bright sunshine.

Slim raised his eyebrows. "So I've heard. You and your dad have a good reputation around here."

Pete nodded, pleased.

"Well," Slim said, shaking Pete's hand. "I'll be in touch if I find anything."

Pete made his way around to his pickup and opened the door as a truck with BRASK FARMS on the door pulled up beside him. A young man Pete didn't recognize jumped out, tipped his cap at Pete, pulled a small spray canister from the bed of the truck, and hurried toward the office.

A FEW MINUTES LATER, when Pete swung into the driveway of Heather Creek Farm, Charlotte stood in the middle of the garden, a hoe in her hand, and her straw hat on her head. She started toward him as he parked his truck. He felt a little anxious and searched her face, afraid she might have a message from Dana.

"Dick Barry called this afternoon," she said as he stepped from his pickup. "The fungus is in his field now too."

The Barrys were to the east of Heather Creek Farm but still along the creek; they'd nearly been flooded out a couple of springs ago. They had a small operation too, although not quite as small as the Maynards'.

Charlotte continued, taking off her gloves as she spoke. "Dad talked with Silas, Frank, and Dick. They're all coming over for coffee tomorrow morning."

"But we don't know anything yet," Pete said. "The extension office was useless, so I went to the college." He didn't need to tell her about stopping by Brask Farms. Slim Stanton seemed like a fine fellow; he'd let them know if the fungus showed up there.

"The extension office and the college? Well, in that case, you made good time."

Pete rolled his eyes, imagining what his dad had been saying for the last couple of hours. "I won't hear back from the ag lab until next week."

Charlotte slapped her gloves together, knocking off the dirt. "I think they still want to get together."

"What time?"

"Nine. Not early."

He nodded. "Any word from Dana?"

Charlotte shook her head. "Have you checked your phone?"

He wanted to roll his eyes. Service was spotty on the farm and along the route to Harding. And no, he hadn't checked it. He wasn't like most of the world that lived by the ring or beep of their cell. Most of the time he forgot he even had one. He took it out of his pocket. He hadn't missed any calls.

"I'll check in with her—and then finish up working the Home Quarter." As he headed back to his pickup, he exhaled loudly. There was never enough time to get everything done that he needed to do. And now he'd have to give up more time tomorrow morning for a bunch of old geezers.

Chapter Four

Saturday morning Charlotte sat at her oak desk with a steaming cup of coffee, a pile of bills, and the bank statement that had come the day before. She straightened her back against the chair and tilted her head to the side, trying to work out the kink in her neck. She took a sip of coffee and then opened up the checkbook register, comparing the entries to the statement. Their wheat was still in the elevator, waiting to be sold. The price had dropped drastically from last year, and she was hoping if they waited a few more weeks the price might go up, but the truth was, it might go down even more.

She hadn't had a check to deposit in months and had been hoping the wheat would have sold by now. She needed to talk with Sam about his tuition bill, which had arrived the day before. She was pretty sure he had the money in his savings account—thanks to his job with Bill's law office. Her preference had been for him to save his money for his last two years of college, when Emily would be going too, but he would need to pay this bill after all.

Her fingers flew across the calculator. She sighed. There was money in savings, but once she started transferring from one account to the other, she knew from experience that they were in a rough spot.

She flipped through the bills and began writing the first check. At least they had enough food—milk from Trudy, fresh vegetables from the garden, fruit from the plum tree, eggs from the chickens, meat in the freezer... They weren't going to starve.

"Char?"

"In the family room," she called out and then shoved the check and the bill into an envelope and sealed it.

"Do we have anything we can serve our guests?" Bob stood in the doorway.

"Coffee—"

"How about a treat?"

Charlotte glanced at her watch. It was 7:30. "I can make an apple crisp." She would use oatmeal, lots of it, and hardly any sugar so Bob could eat it.

"Thanks," he said, settling into his chair.

Charlotte turned her attention back to the bills.

"How do things look?"

She hesitated for a moment. "Okay." She didn't want to rattle him. If he knew how short they were he would probably start complaining about Pete's new house or something else. Or worry more about the soybean crop.

CHARLOTTE PASSED PLATES of apple crisp to the men gathered around the dining room table. Bob sat in his usual place and Pete sat in hers.

"It all seems a little suspicious to me," Silas Maynard said.

"How so?" Pete shoveled a bite of crisp into his mouth.

"Well, we're all downwind from the corporate farm."

"But they don't have the fungus," Pete said, his mouth half full. "I stopped by yesterday."

"Exactly." Silas pushed back in his chair a little. "But we know they're interested in our farms."

"They are?" Pete's fork stopped above his plate.

"Sure. Haven't they approached you about selling?"

Pete shook his head.

"They've approached me," Silas muttered, and then added, "indirectly."

Pete looked at Frank and then Dick. They both shook their heads.

Charlotte realized she was staring at Silas and took the crisp back to the kitchen, putting it on the counter.

"Oh, they want our farms all right," Silas said. Charlotte headed back into the dining room with a fresh pot of coffee. Silas rocked his chair a little. "They want all the farms along Heather Creek."

"What are you getting at?" Pete said as he raised his coffee cup to his mouth.

Silas leaned forward and lowered his voice. "Well, maybe they sent those fungus spores our way, you know, released them into the wind. Or sprayed them directly onto our crops."

Pete yelped a little as he put his coffee cup back on the table. "You're kidding."

Silas shook his finger at Pete. "I wouldn't put it past them. I know they have a lab, and there was a sprayer just outside the office door. I saw both with my own two eyes yesterday afternoon."

"What time?" Pete leaned forward.

"Around five or so. After I finished my day. I decided to do some snooping." He crossed his arms.

"Did you talk to the foreman?"

Silas's face reddened. "No one was around—so I just peeked inside.

Charlotte poured Bob more coffee and then moved on to Frank. Silas's coffee cup was half full, so she topped it off too. He was a quirky guy, but he had helped Bill out of a troubled real-estate deal recently so she knew he meant well.

"Criminal intent seems like a stretch," Pete said, and then he grinned at Silas, who leaned back against his chair with a frown on his face. Pete kept talking. "The lady at the college in Harding had an idea. She said we could start plucking the leaves off."

"One by one?" Bob asked.

"Yep."

Bob hooked his thumbs around his suspenders. "That sounds like an impossible task."

"What did she say it was?" Frank asked. "A fungus? For sure?"

"She said it looked like one," Pete said. "But she was going to do some tests."

Charlotte headed back into the kitchen and put the coffee carafe back in the machine.

"*Psst.* Grandma." Christopher was on the other side of the stove. "Why are all those guys over here?"

"They're just talking about farming."

"On a Saturday morning?"

"Yep."

"Weird," Christopher said. "I can think of lots of other things to do."

Charlotte tousled his head. "What's Sam up to?"

"Sleeping."

Charlotte had told him to set his alarm and not waste the day. "What about Emily?"

"Gathering the eggs."

"Good." Charlotte stepped through the kitchen door onto the mud porch and slipped her boots on.

Silas's loud voice reverberated out of the dining room as she opened the back door. "I'm just saying—" She pulled the door shut behind her. A conspiracy theory was all they needed. She didn't want to think about what would happen if the blight took off, but there was no way in the world that anyone would purposefully infect a crop with a fungus.

"Grandma, where are you going?"

Charlotte turned as Christopher bounded across the lawn behind her.

"To the garden." The day was already warm with the sun now shining above the barn in the eastern sky. A hawk soared over the field, and the horses grazed in the pasture.

"How are my pumpkins?" Christopher slowed as he caught up with her.

Charlotte smiled. "Probably a little bigger than yesterday." They seemed to be growing by the minute now. Christopher had turned the soil in the spring, working in compost and cow manure, creating a perfect mix for supersized pumpkins. His effort had paid off.

Charlotte's row of sunflowers at the far end of the garden bowed gracefully in the slight breeze but seemed to shudder just a little as Emily banged the gate to the chicken coop behind her. She squinted against the morning sun. "Are those guys still yakking it up?"

"Yep," Christopher called out. "I'm going to walk down to the creek. Want to come with me?"

"No." Emily started to march toward the house, the basket swinging.

"Em, careful with those eggs," Charlotte called out. "We don't want them scrambled, not yet."

Her granddaughter scowled a little but slowed her pace. Something was definitely bugging Emily, but Charlotte just wasn't sure what.

A horn honked out on the road. Charlotte stepped to the side of the house and caught a glimpse of the mailman stuffing the mailbox. She waved and then started toward the driveway.

"I'll go get it," Christopher said.

"I'll come with you," Charlotte answered. She needed to stretch her legs; in fact a long walk with Hannah later in the day would be wonderful. Maybe she could spend some time with Emily before then though.

Christopher started to jog ahead, and Toby ran to keep up, barking and turning this way and that, her black, white, and brown fur gleaming in the sunshine. The mail carrier was early; he probably wanted to spend as much of the day with his family as he could. His station wagon disappeared over the crest of the hill, followed by a Brask Farms truck as it passed the grain elevator.

Christopher stopped to poke at a dead bird with a stick. "Don't touch it with your hands," Charlotte said, even though he obviously knew that. "And keep Toby away." She would need to come back with the shovel or send Sam out to get it.

She reached the mailbox and pulled out the collection of magazines, advertisements, and envelopes and then sorted through the items as she walked back up the driveway. Christopher and Toby were jogging ahead. She tucked the mail-order catalogs and advertisements under her arm to deposit in the burn barrel. There was no need to even let the stuff in the house. There wasn't any extra money for shopping, and she didn't want Emily to get any ideas. She thumbed past the phone bill and then stopped at an envelope from the bank, from the branch in Grand Island, not the local one in Bedford.

"Grandma!" Christopher raced toward her.

"What is it?" she called out, quickly placing the envelope with the other mail.

"I'll get the shovel and take care of the dead crow."

"Thank you." She should have thought to ask Christopher to do it. He was perfectly capable.

The letter felt hot in her hand as she quickened her stride across the front lawn. She tossed the advertisements into the barrel at the edge of the yard and entered the house through the front door.

She nearly bumped into Emily as she headed down the hall.

"What's up?" Emily tilted her head.

Charlotte smiled. "Oh, nothing. Christopher found a dead crow out in the driveway though."

"You're kidding." Emily chuckled. "You wouldn't believe what that one guy said—Silas Maynard, right?"

Charlotte nodded as she said, "Lower your voice, sweetie."

Emily began to whisper. "He thinks that big corporate farm is spraying fungus around and poisoning the animals. He's found raccoons, possums, birds—all dead."

"Any livestock?"

"No." Emily raised her eyebrows. "Good point."

Charlotte excused herself. "I have some bills here that I need to put away." She sidestepped into the family room and opened the bills drawer, putting the phone bill inside, and then headed back down the hall to her room with the envelope from the bank.

The men were still talking in the dining room, and chances were that Christopher would stay outside for a while. She stepped into her room, closed the door, and sank down onto her bed. She carefully ran her finger under the seal, opened the envelope, and pulled out a letter written on the bank letterhead.

What had Pete done? The bank expected a balloon payment of ten thousand dollars in—she thought through the days—just about two weeks. She flipped to the second piece of paper, a statement that detailed the loan.

"Char!" Bob's voice carried down the hall. "You in here?" He opened the door.

"Dad!" Pete's voice wasn't far behind.

"How did the meeting go?" Charlotte stood, the letter in her hand.

Bob's face was red. "Silas Maynard says he has proof—"

Pete interrupted. "It's obvious Silas didn't take his meds today."

"Meds?" Charlotte said. "What do you mean?"

Pete shrugged. "He's off his rocker. I've never heard such a bunch of baloney."

"It's not that far-fetched," Bob said.

"Bob?" Charlotte stared at her husband. It wasn't like him to believe such nonsense.

Bob looked at Pete. "I wouldn't put anything past those big farms."

Pete shook his head. "I'm telling you, Slim Stanton seems like a regular guy."

"You didn't see anything suspicious?"

Pete's arms flopped to his sides. "Like a microscope and

a sprayer? Every farm has sprayers, and it's not that out of the ordinary for a big place to have a microscope."

"Why didn't you say something earlier about stopping by there?" Bob's voice rose with each word.

"It's irrelevant."

Charlotte slipped into the hall as Bob and Pete argued. She would talk to Pete later about the loan he apparently had negotiated. He'd either failed to give her and Bob all the details or the *bank* was off its rocker.

CHARLOTTE WATCHED SAM turn off the mower and roll it toward Pete's truck. The lawn looked good; it would need only a few more cuttings before winter set in. Charlotte was thankful to have Sam do the work.

Pete let down the tailgate to his pickup, and together he and Sam lifted the mower into the bed of the truck. "Thanks," Pete said. "This will save me some time. I can fix mine later." His mower had quit on him the night before, and he wanted the house to look sharp because a family who was interested in making an offer was going to take another look the next afternoon.

Sam wiped his hands on the back of his jeans and headed toward the garden where Christopher was weeding his pumpkin patch.

"Pete." Charlotte kept an eye on the boys. "I need to talk to you about the bank loan."

"Now?" He opened the door to his cab.

"Yes." Her eye twitched as she spoke. "We got a notice from the bank today that a ten-thousand-dollar balloon payment is due in just over two weeks."

"What?" He sank down on the seat of his truck, his legs sticking out the open door.

Charlotte nodded. "You never said anything about a balloon payment, especially not in September."

"The bank never said anything about a balloon payment either." He threw up his hands. "This is outrageous! It's a mistake. I'll straighten it out on Monday."

Charlotte hoped with all her heart it *was* a mistake.

"Does Dad know?"

"I haven't had a chance to tell him."

"Could you wait? Until I straighten this out?"

Charlotte didn't like the idea of keeping anything from Bob, but it would be best if Pete worked this out on his own, especially if he was going to take over the farm soon.

She nodded, squinting against the late afternoon sun. "I'll wait." She would go through her files and find their copy of the paperwork.

"It'll be fine." Pete swung his legs into the pickup. "I promise."

Charlotte walked toward the garden as Pete drove away. Sam sat on the lawn, tossing clumps of cut grass at his little brother. Charlotte kneeled down beside him. "How is school going?"

"Fine." He twirled a blade of grass between his fingers.

"Your tuition bill came."

"How much is it?"

"Six hundred something." Charlotte knew he'd gotten a two-hundred-dollar scholarship. That helped. "Can you pay it this term? Hopefully we'll be able to help you next term, after we sell the crops."

Sam brushed the grass from his hands. "I guess I could. But I'm thinking about not working for Uncle Bill much longer. I don't have much time with school and driving back and forth. I haven't put in many hours in the last couple of weeks."

"It would be good to find a new job before you quit. Make sure you leave your options open with Bill; maybe you could work for him over Christmas break and next summer. Ask him about that."

Sam nodded.

She patted his shoulder. "Thanks for paying the tuition. That's a big help." She stood.

"Grandma, are we doing okay?" Sam asked.

She stooped down a little. "Yes. It's just that farm prices are falling, and you know, we don't get a steady monthly income."

Sam nodded.

"But I don't want you to worry." She paused. "Things are a little tight right now; that's all."

ALL THROUGH THE church service the next morning, Charlotte's mind kept wandering. As Pastor Nathan spread his open Bible on the pulpit and asked everyone to join him in prayer, Charlotte tried not to think about their money woes.

"What is troubling *you* today?" Pastor Nathan boomed. He wasn't a big person, but his voice was the voice of a much larger man. "Have you talked with God about it? Told Him your worries?"

Charlotte sat up straighter. She hadn't prayed about the bank loan; she'd been too busy worrying about it.

"God wants us to talk to Him."

Charlotte gripped her Bible tighter, feeling as if Pastor Nathan was speaking directly to her as he pushed his glasses up on the bridge of his nose.

"Sometimes we seem to enjoy worrying. We fret about our jobs. About our children. About our finances."

Charlotte's gaze fell past Pastor Nathan to the cross on

the wall. She had looked for the loan documentation the evening before but hadn't found it, and now she wondered if she should go to the bank with Pete first thing tomorrow morning. She wasn't sure if she could trust him to handle such an important matter.

There was enough in savings to pay the balloon payment, but if the soybean crop failed, they wouldn't have enough to pay off the entire loan—all forty thousand dollars—without dipping into her and Bob's retirement savings, which wasn't just for them now. They would need it to get the kids through college too.

She turned her head to the left. Emily sat a row ahead with Ashley. Christopher sat next to Charlotte on the right and then Sam. Both had their heads down, staring at their bulletins. Just past them were Pete and Dana.

What had she and Bob been thinking to let Pete sign for the loan?

As Pastor Nathan began his sermon, she thought of how well the kids were doing. Sure, there would always be ups and downs, but she felt that even the kids believed now that they belonged at Heather Creek Farm. They hadn't heard much from Kevin since his graduation card to Sam, postmarked from Texas last May. It seemed he wouldn't interfere with the kids, so maybe that had helped them feel more settled too. Her eyes teared as she wondered what would happen to them if they lost the farm.

As Christopher leaned his head against her shoulder, she put her arm around him and chastised herself for thinking such a thing. They'd been in bad spots before and always pulled through. But they hadn't been old then.

"Today," Pastor Nathan said, concluding his sermon,

"whatever you're worrying about, take it to God. Tell Him about it."

Charlotte groaned inside and silently prayed, *Dear Lord, I need Your help on this one.*

AFTER CHURCH, Pete yanked the mower out of the back of his truck, pulling up on the handle. It landed on its front tires, and then he lowered it on the driveway.

Randy, the real estate agent, was showing the house again in an hour. That gave him plenty of time to mow but not to edge.

He decided to start in the front and pushed the machine down the sidewalk. What he really wanted was a nap, a quick escape from thinking about the fungus, the looming bank loan, and everything that needed to be done before harvest. To be honest, he couldn't really remember what he'd negotiated with the bank. He was sure he'd remember a ten-thousand-dollar payment though. Mom had given him some guidelines—he remembered that—and he thought he'd done exactly what she'd asked. He was sure he'd given her the paperwork afterward.

He reached for the pull on the lawn mower just as Dana called out his name. The screen door banged, and she hurried down the steps. "They went ahead and made an offer—said they don't need to see it again. You can wait until it cools off to cut the grass."

He let go of the cord and stood. Not mowing on a hot Sunday afternoon sounded good to him.

"Randy's on his way over with the papers." Dana was practically doing a jig on the sidewalk. All along their

Realtor had been assuring them that the house would sell, even in the tight economy.

He left the mower where it was and rushed toward her. She threw her arms around his neck, laughing. "We can finish the new house now and decorate the nursery."

He lifted her off her feet and spun her around.

Ten minutes later they sat at the dining room table with Randy. "They're a couple with one daughter. First-time buyers. They love the house."

"Enough to offer full price?" Pete asked.

Randy smiled. "Not quite—five thousand less."

Without even glancing at Pete, Dana said, "We'll take it."

Chapter Five

Monday morning, Sam sat at a desk in the computer lab at Central Community College in Grand Island. He had twenty minutes to rework his essay and print it out before his English comp class began. He clicked the keys to open the Word document.

Next to him a girl with carrot red hair pushed back her chair. "Hey," she called out to the techie at the desk, "were you going to help me today or next week?"

"I'll be there in a minute." The guy didn't look up as he stared at the computer screen on his desk. He wore a black sweatshirt and had his hair pulled back into a thin ponytail; a rod pierced through his eyebrow.

The girl exhaled loudly. Her skin was smooth, not all freckly like a lot of people with red hair. Her dark brown eyes flashed.

"What's up?" Sam asked her.

"I can't get my document to print."

"Let me take a look."

She shot a mean look at the techie, who now had his phone out and was sending a text message, and then turned toward Sam. "Why not?" She stood, and he took her chair.

Sam zipped through the printing commands. Nothing happened. The girl was looking over his shoulder and making him nervous. He clicked on the printer setup. Nothing was installed. He reinstalled the center printer, clicked back to her document, and hit PRINT again.

She hurried over to the table of printers and pulled her papers from one of the bins. Then she turned toward Sam. "Thanks."

He nodded, returned to the computer he had been working at, and refocused on his essay.

"Hey, I'm Lyla." The girl extended her hand.

"Sam." He took it quickly. Her bones felt fragile, as if they might break if he squeezed too hard.

"Are you this quick with computers generally?" She swung her backpack over one shoulder.

"Sometimes."

"I'm the editor of the school newspaper. Normally I'd be working in our lab, but we're having technical problems and our techie just quit." She took her phone from her pocket, read a text, glanced at the guy at the desk, and then turned back to Sam. "You interested in a job?"

"I might be," Sam said.

"Want to come check out the lab—say, later this afternoon?"

"Sure. I'm done with class at three."

"Perfect," Lyla said. "I'll meet you there." She was as tiny as her hands and had a sassy attitude he liked—but also scared him.

He glanced at the time on the computer. Now he had ten minutes to finish his essay. As he reread the first paragraph he realized he had no idea where the newspaper office was. He turned toward the techie and asked him.

The guy slipped his phone into his sweatshirt pocket and chuckled. "You're a sucker if you take that job."

Sam shrugged.

"Lyla's trouble." He stretched and yawned. "But you'll figure that out soon enough. The office is on the third floor of this building, at the very end of the south hall. But I'm telling you, she's a slave driver."

"How do you know?" Sam asked, already drifting back to his essay.

"I used to work for her. I just started in here yesterday."

AFTER CALCULUS, Sam headed up the stairwell to the third floor. The guy in the computer lab had looked sketchy and not like a reliable source. Sure, he could see Lyla as being one of those bossy girls who tried really hard to control everything and everyone, but a part-time job at the college would work out great. It would allow him to quit working for Bill while classes were in session. Working at the college would be a whole lot more convenient than working in River Bend.

He reached the landing, pushed through the heavy fire door, and headed down the hall. The door at the very end was open, and he stepped inside. A table with three Mac computers was pushed up against the far wall, and a printer, with a tangle of wires around it, sat on the floor; stacks of newspapers were piled under the windows.

"Hello," Sam called out, but no one answered. On a desk on the opposite wall from the computers was Lyla's backpack. She had to be somewhere nearby. He poked his head back into the hall. There she was, coming out of the women's restroom, her face all red and puffy. Sam ducked back into the room and hurried over to the computers. He didn't know much about Macs; he'd messed around with Jason Vink's laptop during youth group a couple of times, making PowerPoint presentations and things like that, but that was all. He headed over to the printer and started following the cables. He could do some untangling.

"Oh, hi." Lyla paused in the doorway for just a moment and then walked slowly across the room. "Have you worked with Macs before?"

"A little."

"We use InDesign, but of course you wouldn't have to do anything with that except maybe reinstall it now and then."

Sam leaned against a chair. "I can do that."

"Right now none of the computers are online. I don't know what happened, and Russell—"

"Russell?"

"He was the jerk in the computer lab this morning."

"Oh."

"I think he took them offline on purpose. That was why I couldn't print out my paper up here. I couldn't get into my e-mail account to download it after the teacher sent it back asking for corrections."

Sam sat down in the chair and moved the mouse around until the screen came alive. He clicked on the Internet browser icon. Sure enough, the program had been uninstalled. He clicked through the reinstallation, and in a minute it was up again.

"Cool," Lyla said. Her eyes brightened a little. "So, do you want the job?"

"Tell me what I would be doing exactly."

"Technical support. Seeing to the hardware—making the

printer work, like you did this morning. Installing software. That sort of thing."

"Could I think about it overnight?" Maybe he could stop by and see Jason Vink and get some pointers. Or maybe he would just Google Macs and InDesign and everything else he needed to know.

Lyla scowled. "Sure. Stop by tomorrow afternoon and let me know."

"Okay." He got out of class at one on Tuesdays; he could stick around another hour.

"Oh, and you'd need to update our website after each issue of the newspaper comes out," Lyla said. "But that's really easy—even Russell could do that."

It didn't sound easy to Sam, but he was sure he could learn that too.

SAM SLIPPED HIS BACKPACK off his shoulder onto a dining room chair and headed straight for the family room when he arrived home. He came to an abrupt halt in the middle of the room—Grandma and Pete were huddled over the desk with a stack of papers between them.

"I know I gave you the paperwork," Pete said.

"If you did, I would have filed it." Grandma stood up straight. "And besides, you said you were going to call the bank today."

Uh-oh, not more money problems. Sam slipped onto the computer chair and swiveled around, facing his grandmother and uncle.

"I got busy," Pete said. "I'll call now."

Grandma pointed at her watch. "It's too late. They're closed. We're going to go together tomorrow." She turned and halted at the sight of Sam as Pete fled into the dining room. "When did you get home?"

"Just now."

Her face was flushed, and the sleeves of her blouse were rolled to her elbows.

"I have some research to do," he said.

"The room's all yours." Grandma started to the kitchen and then stopped. "What are you working on?"

Sam shrugged. "All sorts of stuff." He didn't want to tell her about the job possibility; she would ask too many questions. He sat down in the chair and clicked online. "Grandma," he called out.

"Yes." She hadn't gone far.

"Do you think Jason Vink would help me with something?"

"Like what?" She was behind him now.

"Oh, I just have some questions for him." Sam glanced over his shoulder. Grandma was beaming. She probably thought he had some religious concerns or something.

"Oh, sweetie, I'm sure he will. Just give him a call."

Sam nodded. First he needed to see what he could find online. Then he'd call Jason Vink.

A half hour later, Sam was sitting in the youth pastor's office at the church, looking at his Mac laptop.

"So what do you need to know?"

"How to load software, figure out the hardware, that sort of thing," Sam explained.

Jason stood beside his desk. "So you can . . . ?"

"Get a job with the school newspaper." Sam leaned back against the old beater couch with the stuffing coming out of the arms.

"And you think I can teach you all that in a half hour?" Jason looked at his cell. "Because that's all the time I have before I need to get home and help with dinner."

"I just need an introduction." Sam squirmed a little, trying to get comfortable.

Jason shook his head. "Sounds to me like you're trying to fudge your way into a job."

"No." Sam sat up straighter. "Honestly, I'm good with computers. I'm sure I can do this.

Jason gave him one of those deep looks, and Sam tried to keep still.

"I don't have InDesign." Jason picked up his laptop and plopped down on the couch beside Sam. "But Rick down at the *Bedford Leader* does, and he never leaves the place until seven or eight unless he's off to a meeting or a game. You could stop by before you go home; if he doesn't have time he'll let you know." Jason chuckled a little. "Those newspaper people are usually pretty honest."

Sam nodded. That certainly seemed to be the case with Lyla.

"Too bad you don't want to learn about iMovie; I've been messing around with that lately, and it's really cool."

Sam smiled. He didn't think he'd have any need for iMovie at the college newspaper. "I can show you the basics of a Mac, but you're definitely going to need more info than this to support a newspaper. Believe me, you don't want to misrepresent yourself. That's not going to help anyone." Jason scooted closer to Sam, clicked into iTunes, selected a Christian rock artist, edged the MacBook between them, and clicked on About this Mac. "Okay, stay with me. It's going to be a fast trip, and I'll teach you what I can, but it's up to you to be completely honest with whoever does the hiring and tell them exactly what your skills are."

Sam leaned forward, his eyes glued to the screen.

HALF AN HOUR LATER, armed with that basic Macintosh introduction, Sam ran over to the *Bedford Leader* office, checking the time on his cell phone as he stopped in front of the brick building. It was 6:25. He hurried to the door and pushed it open, his palms sweaty.

"Hello," he called out as he walked into the office. No one answered. It wasn't as if he wasn't acquainted with Rick Barnes. In fact, the editor had featured Sam in an article when he had rescued Daisy Davis from Heather Creek, and he also wrote about him when he was kicking for the football team. Hopefully the man would remember him. Sam called out hello again.

"Be right there," came Rick's voice from the back of the building.

Sam looked at the pictures hanging on the office walls, the old-time photos of downtown Bedford with Model-T cars and ladies in white dresses and parasols. He moved on to the farming photos of men wearing suspenders and straw hats, all posed around a threshing machine. Grandma had said that was how her grandparents used to harvest their wheat. Boy, that was a long time ago. It made Grandma seem ancient. He stopped in front of a framed copy of the first edition of the *Bedford Leader*. He squinted to read the year. 1878.

"Sam Slater." Rick Barnes was coming toward him, his hand outstretched. "What can I do to help you?"

Sam shook his hand and then explained that he was hoping to learn a little about web design.

Rick scratched his head. "I could show you on Wednesday, but tonight and tomorrow I'm trying to get the paper out."

Sam's face must have given away his disappointment because Rick started rummaging on a desk that was covered with clutter—legal pads, scraps of paper, newspapers, pens, and dirty coffee cups—and pulled out a book. "You can have this. I have several copies floating around here. It will give you the basics."

"Thanks," Sam said, sure he could learn what he needed from the book about how to maintain a website.

Chapter Six

Pete pulled the cord on the lawn mower, eyeing the sky. It was growing dark quickly. He figured he had twenty minutes to get the lawn mowed before he wouldn't be able to see. It wasn't as important now that the house had sold, but still he wanted to keep things looking tidy. Besides, Dad had asked twice when he was going to return the lawn mower, even though Pete had only had the mower since Saturday evening, less than forty-eight hours.

He couldn't remember why he hadn't mowed Sunday evening. It seemed like he was as tired as Dana lately. And more forgetful. He couldn't believe he'd spaced out about calling the bank.

He started in the front along the flowerbed. Someone needed to clip the dying dahlia blossoms. The lavender ones had turned brown and looked pathetic. Dana had taken care of the flowers all summer, but he didn't think she'd even noticed the yard since school started. In fact, right now she was napping on the couch. He sure hoped things were better for her after the first trimester ended; he felt bad that she had to go to work when she felt poorly. He whipped the mower back around and headed toward the porch. Thunderclouds gathered in the western sky.

They certainly had been having their share of storms lately, more than usual.

He had remembered to call the Harding College ag department in the late afternoon, but Dr. Anderson wasn't in and the man who answered the phone couldn't help. He would need to remember to call again in the morning. He pushed the mower onto the walkway and turned it sharply to head back the other way. Just as he did, Dana came out of the house, the phone in her hand, pointing it at him. She was barefoot, and her eyes still had a sleepy look to them.

He turned off the mower and wiped his palms on his jeans.

"It's someone from the college," Dana said, meeting him at the bottom of the steps.

He took the phone and said hello.

"I confirmed what you suspected." It was Dr. Anderson. "It is a fungus. A mutation of what you probably sprayed for."

"Are there any sprays available for it?"

"Not that I know of," she said.

"Have you seen this before?" Pete asked.

"No. This is new, but it's not unusual for a fungus to mutate."

Pete assured her that he'd heard of fungus mutating. "Just not on my farm," he added. He looked up to see if Dana was still on the porch. She was sitting on the swing. He felt a little funny saying "my farm" and wondered if she had noticed. "Any advice on how to deal with it—since spraying again won't help?"

"Like I said on Friday, you can go plant by plant and pick

the affected leaves. It's a hassle, but it won't significantly affect your yield."

He didn't need her to add that the fungus could though.

"How much is it apt to spread if we don't do anything?"

"It depends on how much moisture you get between now and harvest. Typically, it wouldn't spread much, but as you know, when it comes to farming, nothing is typical."

Pete agreed.

"Call me if you have any other questions," she said and then added that she would log the fungus for future reference.

"Wait," Pete said. "I have another question." He stepped toward the street. "Is there any way—" He felt ridiculous even asking. "Is it possible that the fungus could be spread, you know, maliciously?"

She laughed.

"Okay, I'm not serious, but I had to ask. One of our neighbors has this conspiracy theory going."

"Well, sure, in theory it's possible. Someone could cultivate and spray it on purpose. For the record, I've never heard of that sort of thing though," she said. She laughed again.

"Okay." Pete wanted nothing more than to end the conversation. "Thanks," he muttered.

He walked up the steps and handed Dana the phone. "It's a fungus."

"I gathered," Dana said. "What are you going to do?"

"I'm not sure." He tried to smile. "I guess I'll finish mowing the lawn before it gets dark." He bent down and kissed her on the cheek. And try not to worry. Or become overwhelmed with everything they needed to do, like pack up the house. Now the contractor would have to work like mad to do the finishing work before the sale of this house closed, or they would have to decide where to live until the house was finished. Maybe with Grandma Maxie. She had more room than Mom and Dad did.

Later, he'd finished the front yard and was mowing the back in the near dark when Dana appeared on the back porch, the phone in her hand again. She motioned to him as she talked. He almost asked her to take a message, but she seemed upset. He quickly cut the mower's engine and hurried up the stairs.

"Is everything okay?" he mouthed.

"It's Randy," Dana mouthed and then said, "Here, I'm going to have you talk to Pete."

He took the phone.

"Pete. I have bad news." Randy's voice was low. "The buyers backed out."

"Seriously?"

"They decided to keep renting for now."

"But mortgage rates are so low. And the house is listed at such a good price."

"Exactly. That's why I think we'll have another buyer in no time."

"Why did the buyers back out?"

"I'm not sure."

"What about the earnest money?"

"It's only been twenty-four hours since the offer; they get it back."

Pete tried to remember the buyers' story. A husband and wife and daughter. The husband drove a truck or something like that. And the wife worked in Harding at the hospital. "So what do we do?"

"Take the SALE PENDING sign down. Have an open house next Sunday. Make sure things look tidy."

Pete put his arm around Dana and pulled her head against his shoulder. "We really need it to sell so we can finish financing the house we're building."

"Don't worry, it will sell," Randy said. "I'll advertise the open house from two to four on Sunday. Just make sure everything is tip-top."

"Right." Pete said good-bye and handed Dana the phone. "Back to the drawing board." He tried, but failed, to sound upbeat.

"What if it doesn't sell?"

"It will." Pete gave her another squeeze. "I'll be just another minute; I need to finish the lawn before it's completely dark." He started down the steps and then turned. "Hey, would you turn on the porch light?"

She nodded and, looking dejected, went back into the house. A moment later the light came on.

Pete practically ran as he pushed the mower. What a day. He rushed through the rest of the mowing and then wheeled the machine around to the driveway and hoisted it up into the bed of his truck. Next he grabbed the clippers off the workbench in the garage and headed to the front yard, zipping through the dying dahlia and gladiolus blooms, lopping off each head.

"Pete."

He raised his head. Dana was standing on the porch, still barefoot. "I thought you were coming in."

"I'm just tidying up since the house is going back on the market. I'll be there in a minute."

She sighed and stepped back into the house, the screen door banging behind her.

It was completely dark as he tried to lift up the edge of the SALE PENDING notice on the FOR SALE sign with his thumbnail. As he worked at it, he heard a crash of thunder and raised his head toward Heather Creek Farm. Lightning streaked across the sky, briefly illuminating the dark, heavy clouds that released sheets of rain on the horizon. Thunder rumbled, and then another bolt of lightning crashed.

"Pete, come inside." Dana stood behind the screen door.

"After I cover the mower with a tarp," he said, heading toward the pickup, overcome with exhaustion.

CHARLOTTE QUICKLY CLOSED the kitchen window against the rain and then stepped to the back door. Emily was hurrying across the yard, holding the empty kitchen-scraps bucket over her head. Beyond her the chickens fluttered in their coop, their usual bedtime routine disturbed by Emily and the crashing thunder.

Emily ran faster and then fell through the mudroom door, panting. "That lightning's close!" Rain dripped from her face.

Charlotte took the bucket. "The storm is right overhead. Get a towel and dry off."

"I'm going to take a shower." Emily kicked off her tennis shoes and hurried through the kitchen.

Charlotte peeked into the dining room. Sam sat at the dining room table reading a book on computers—funny, since he wasn't taking a computer class—and Christopher was hunched over his math homework.

Charlotte stepped into the family room where Bob watched the nightly news. A segment about foreclosures blared too loudly as she sat down at the desk to look through her financial files again.

"What are you up to?" Bob asked, leaning forward in his chair.

"Oh, just looking," she said, and then put the file back in the drawer. She would look later in the evening, after Bob had gone to bed. She moved to the computer desk. She might as well check her e-mail.

Her inbox popped onto the screen with waiting mail that included a squash soup recipe from Hannah and a newsletter from the high school. She sent Hannah a quick thank-you for the recipe and then read the newsletter. The open house later this week was already on the family calendar because Emily had written it down the first day of school.

She closed her e-mail and stared at the screen. Lots of people kept all of their financial records on their computer, even paid their loans over the Internet. Maybe it was time that she updated. It would be so much easier to check, and she wouldn't be relying on Pete's confidence that he had given her all of the paperwork.

Chapter Seven

Emily slumped against the vinyl seat and yawned. Riding the bus was getting really old, even though it was only three weeks into the school year. She took out her American history book and yawned again, opening it to the chapter on the Revolutionary War.

She stared at a drawing of George and Martha Washington. Emily really didn't get men's fashions back then. What was up with the wigs and tights? She liked Martha's gown, though, with the high waist and all, even if it did make her look pregnant. She yawned a third time. In no time Aunt Dana would be showing, and then things would be even more awkward at school.

Emily flipped the page to an image of George Washington on a horse, a stallion that looked to her like he was twenty hands high. He kind of looked like Hunter's horse, Rambo.

The bus lurched to a stop, and three little kids boarded and sat in the empty seat in front of Emily.

"Hey, stop that!" It was Christopher's voice coming from the back of the bus.

Emily turned around. Justin had Christopher in a headlock.

"I said knock it off." Christopher's voice wasn't as loud, and his face was turning red up to his blond hairline.

"Hey!" Emily half stood.

"Sit down please," the bus driver said.

Emily faced forward and locked on the driver's eyes in the rearview mirror. "Justin has Christopher by the head."

The driver braked, and Emily fell forward, accidentally knocking her hand against the back of the head of the little boy in front of her. "Sorry." She sat down in her seat.

"Justin! Knock it off right now," the driver belted out, glaring at Justin in the mirror.

Justin let go of Christopher, but as the driver accelerated again, he knuckled Christopher's head and said, "You'd better watch it, Slater. Your sister isn't always going to be around to save your—"

Emily glared at him, and Justin stepped back across the aisle to his seat but kept his eyes on her.

Emily spun away from him on the vinyl bench. There was no reason to give such a little twit an audience.

EMILY COULDN'T HELP STARING at Aunt Dana, who sat at the teachers' table during lunch. Her aunt looked as if she hadn't slept last night; her eyes were puffy. She wore a pair of wrinkled slacks, and the sleeves of her shirt were rolled up.

"Hey." Lily Cunningham slid her tray onto the table next to Emily and said, "Did you hear about Isabella's dad?"

Ashley, who sat across from Emily, put her hand up as if trying to stop Lily, but it was too late.

"He got arrested night before last. For drunken—"

"Lily." Ashley's voice was low but firm.

"He caused an accident out on the Harding Highway," Lily whispered.

Emily spotted Isabella in the lunch line, picking up a carton of milk. She'd missed the day before and hadn't been her usual rambunctious self in the hall before school. She made eye contact with Emily and waved, balancing her tray with one hand as she walked toward the girls.

"Here she comes." Emily leaned forward.

"Sit here," Ashley called out to Isabella, patting the chair beside her.

A moment later, Isabella settled into the chair.

No one spoke for a moment, but then Isabella blew the wrapper to her straw straight at Emily, pelting her forehead. Emily yelped, and Isabella laughed. "What's with everyone today? Why so serious?"

Emily frowned and rubbed her forehead.

Ashley smiled sweetly at Isabella and then asked the group, "Is everyone caught up with their reading? We're supposed to be on page 94."

Isabella groaned loudly.

"You were home all day yesterday," Lily said. "You should be done with the book by now."

"I'm going to pretend like I didn't hear that." Isabella had a hurt look on her face as she picked up her carton and then took a sip through the straw.

Emily didn't want to comment that she was only on page seventy.

"How about Mrs. Stevenson's—" Ashley was always so careful to get the right name, "—question about benevolence?"

"I don't even know what that means," Isabella wailed.

"To be kind," Ashley explained.

"So why doesn't she just say that?"

"Because we're juniors in high school." Emily wasn't feeling benevolent at all. "We can handle four-syllable words."

Isabella glared at her, and Emily shrank back a little. Ashley, always the peacemaker, said, "I've been thinking about Atticus and how benevolent he is toward Tom Robinson when he goes to the courthouse."

Emily remembered that scene from the movie but hadn't gotten that far in the book. "I think that's past where we're supposed to have read for today."

Ashley blushed. "You're right. I ended up reading the whole thing last night. I couldn't put it down."

"Tell me what I need to know for today so I don't look like an idiot in class," Isabella said.

"How far have you read?" Ashley asked.

"Just a couple of chapters."

"Has Walter gone home to eat dinner with Scout yet?"

Isabella shook her head. Emily couldn't believe how Ashley bent over backward to help the girl. She scanned the cafeteria again. Troy was in the back of the line, holding an empty tray in his hand.

"Well, Scout is kind to Walter," Ashley said. Emily wrinkled her nose. Scout beat Walter up and then humiliated him at dinner.

"Don't you think?" Ashley looked straight at Emily.

"Well," she answered, "she tried to be kind, 'cause, you know, that's what her dad wanted."

"That's a good point," Ashley said, and then started asking Isabella exactly where she was in the story.

Emily wondered if she had learned to be benevolent. Grandma certainly tried to teach that. So had her mom. She couldn't remember her father ever teaching her anything. She sighed. Well, at least her dad wasn't as bad as Isabella's. He'd never been arrested or hurt anyone else. At least she didn't think so.

"Hey." Troy stood behind Emily.

"Hi," she said, turning around in her chair.

"Can I join you?" he asked.

"Um..." Emily stood and grabbed her tray. "How about if we sit over there?" She pointed to the far corner of the cafeteria. She needed a break.

Troy grinned and stepped aside, letting her lead the way.

AFTER SCHOOL, Emily stood on the steps of the school with Troy, aware of the heat of the concrete seeping through the soles of her strappy sandals. A trickle of sweat rolled down the back of her knee, and she pushed her skirt against it, embarrassed at the thought of it dripping down her leg. "I'd better get going," Troy said, "or I'll be late for work."

Emily squinted in the distance at the school bus. "Yeah," she said. "I'd better go too."

They walked to the bottom of the steps and said goodbye. She watched him for a second as he sauntered toward his truck, and then she hurried toward the bus.

"Emily!" She turned back, thinking it was Troy calling her, but it wasn't. "Emily!" The voice was louder, and it was coming from the street, not the parking lot. Beyond the bus, on the other side of the street, stood her father, waving both his hands at her. Her mouth fell open, and her stomach dropped to her feet.

She glanced around quickly, hoping no one else saw him. Then she made her way through the parking lot toward him, waving her hand at waist level, hoping he would stop yelling her name; but he called out "Emily!" again.

Her heart raced as she crossed the street, and then it lurched when she saw Christopher sitting in the passenger seat of the old brown sedan.

"Emily." Dad's face was leaner and longer than last time they'd seen him. He wore jeans and a black T-shirt, and his forehead was scrunched and wrinkled even though he was smiling. "It's so good to see you. What has it been? Six months?"

"Nine," Emily answered. Boy, the guy couldn't get anything right. She turned sideways and gave him a half hug. "What are you doing here?"

He squeezed her shoulder. "I'm going to Harding on a job lead." His voice seemed strange, as if he was trying really hard to sound lighthearted. "I thought I'd give you a ride home, keep you from having to ride that old thing." He nodded across the street toward the bus.

"Oh, I don't mind riding the bus." As she spoke the driver pushed open his side window.

"I'm taking off," he called out to Emily.

"Wait!" She turned to Christopher. "Come on." She opened the car door.

"No, Dad said he'd give us a ride."

She turned back to her father. "Did you get permission from Grandma?"

"For?"

"To give us a ride."

Kevin half grimaced, half smiled. "That's ridiculous." He stepped across the street, looking up at the bus driver. "I'll take the kids home," he said. "I'm their dad." His voice swelled with pride.

The driver waved, a big smile on his face. "In that case, no problem."

Emily groaned as she climbed into the backseat. Grandma wasn't going to be happy.

"How about if we stop for a Coke first?" He started the motor and rested his arm on the frame of the window. Obviously the car didn't have air-conditioning.

"We should get out to the farm," Emily said. "We have homework, right, Christopher?"

"I don't have much."

"We could get a Coke at the grocery store and then go to the park."

Emily put her hand to her forehead.

"Sounds good." Christopher turned to Emily, smiling.

She shook her head. Grandma was going to freak.

Chapter Eight

"You're saying we need to go to the Grand Island branch?" Charlotte said, clutching her purse as she sat in Jerome Sanders's office at the Bedford branch of Great Plains State Bank.

"That's right," Jerome said. "All of our farm loans have been transferred there." He shifted in his leather chair. "We're trying to streamline the process and provide more oversight."

Charlotte pursed her lips. It sounded like the bank had fallen on hard times too.

"Um." Pete scooted forward on his chair. "Someone—maybe me—seems to have misplaced our paperwork on the loan."

Jerome smiled. "You can get another copy. No problem. Just call Grand Island and make a request." He stood. "And good luck." He shook Pete's hand and then Charlotte's.

As they stepped into the sunshine, Pete led the way toward his truck. "That wasn't so bad."

"Except we still need to get over to Grand Island."

"I'll call and ask them to send a copy of the loan." Pete opened his door.

Charlotte shook her head as she climbed into the pickup. "Pete." She slammed her door. "They already sent us a copy."

"But maybe they made a mistake."

She leaned against the seat and closed her eyes. Maybe a mix-up had happened when the loans were transferred from the Bedford branch. Or maybe Pete hadn't read the fine print. Her head began to pound as Pete turned onto the highway toward home. As they passed the corporate farm, the pickup began to veer toward the shoulder of the road as Pete craned his neck, probably taking in the late-model tractor plowing the field nearest the highway. She started to reprimand him, but he caught himself.

"I didn't want to worry you more." Pete looked straight ahead as he drove. "But you need to know this. The buyers backed out. Our house hasn't sold after all."

"Oh, Pete." Boy, when it rained it poured.

"The Realtor said not to worry; he's sure we'll have another buyer in no time."

"What happened?"

"Something's going on with the husband's job. Dana thinks it's a family who has a daughter in her class; the girl was absent yesterday. Go figure. But anyway, it's on the market again."

"Oh dear," Charlotte said again.

"That's an understatement." Pete scowled.

"Did you hear back from Harding College?" She'd forgotten to ask him on the way into town.

Pete swallowed. "Just that it's a fungus. A mutated one."

"What exactly does that mean?"

Pete shrugged and then spoke, "That we're..." He paused. "In a bad spot, no pun intended."

"Did they say anything else?"

"Like?"

"Oh, I don't know. What might cause it, that sort of thing."

"It seems to be related to all the rain we've been getting but—" He paused for a moment, glanced toward her, and then turned back to the road. "As ludicrous as it sounds, she did admit that someone could purposefully spread it."

"Pete." Charlotte shook her head. The whole conspiracy theory was absolutely ridiculous.

"I'm just passing on information."

"Well, don't tell Dad, okay? Or Silas Maynard. It's too much."

"What if it wasn't the corporate farm?" Pete said. "What if it was one of the neighbors?"

"Oh, goodness," she said. "That's even more ridiculous."

Pete sighed. "Anyway, we're in a pickle all the way around."

Charlotte nodded. "Well, it doesn't do any good to worry," she said, but her words rang hollow. They were silent as they passed the squash-colored school bus just before Hannah's house. Then Charlotte said, "Drop me off at our mailbox." She'd wait for the children and walk up the drive with them. "But call the Grand Island branch as soon as you get to the house. We need to talk to whoever is in charge of the farm loans."

Pete frowned but nodded as he turned into the lane and then stopped. "See you at the house." She climbed from the truck and brushed her hands against the thighs of her slacks. Thankfully, there was only an advertisement in the mailbox today, no bills. She looked at it absentmindedly as she waited. A minute later the bus stopped and the door swung open. She peered up the bus steps toward the driver.

"Their dad was at the school," he called down. "Said he was bringing them home. Aren't they here?"

"Oh." Charlotte hopped a little as she spoke, and her purse banged against her leg. *Their dad*, she thought to herself swallowing her shock. "Well." She turned toward the house, as if she could see the children inside, and then faced the driver. "I just got here myself. I had my son drop me off to wait for them. I'm sure they're at the house."

She waved to him and turned on her heels, speed-walking down the lane. A moment later she was running. She passed the barn and the shed and then rounded the lawn. Her car was in its usual spot, but Kevin's red pickup wasn't anywhere in sight. Maybe he had dropped them off. Toby peeked her head out of her doghouse and then bounded toward Charlotte.

"Are they here, girl?" She was out of breath as she flung open the back door and stumbled into the kitchen. "Emily! Christopher!" she yelled. "Are you here?"

She rushed to the family room, where Bob shifted in his chair, rubbing his eyes.

"Are the children here?" Sweat covered her forehead, and her heart pounded in her chest.

"Char, what's going on?" Bob sat up straight.

"Kevin picked up the kids at school." She rushed past him to the staircase, yelling their names again.

"Kevin? Isn't he in Texas?" Bob stepped into the hallway. "They're not here. They must have stopped somewhere."

Charlotte collapsed onto the bottom stair and leaned her head against the newel post. "Or left." She searched Bob's face. "What if he's taken the children?"

CHARLOTTE HUNG UP the phone. The elementary school receptionist had taken a report and said the principal would talk to the bus driver as soon as he finished his route. Obviously Bedford School District's policy hadn't been followed.

"What now?" Bob said.

"I'll try Emily's cell phone." Charlotte said. As she dialed the number she said a prayer that the call would go through. It didn't.

"Now we should call the police and put out an Amber alert." She started to dial 9-1-1.

"Char, wait," Bob said. "What if he took them out for ice cream or something? Maybe they'll be here any minute."

She held the phone in midair. "What if he's already in Kansas? What if we never see the kids again?"

Toby began to bark, and Charlotte ran to the back door. A brown sedan pulled up next to her car. She hurried out, still clutching the phone.

It was Kevin, his head hanging out the driver's window.

"Are the children with you?" Her voice was shrill.

He nodded, a wide smile on his face.

Charlotte's legs nearly collapsed under her as Christopher and Emily climbed from the car, each holding a bottle of soda.

"We were going to go to the park," Christopher said, "but it was too hot."

Kevin climbed from the car and then waved at Bob, who came through the door after Charlotte.

"Grandma," Emily said quietly, "are you upset?"

Charlotte turned toward Kevin. "You're not authorized to pick up the kids from school."

"Oh, it was fine," he said. "I talked to the bus driver."

"No, you don't understand. You're not on the list."

"What list?" He laughed. "I'm their father."

"I told him he wasn't supposed to," Emily said.

Charlotte put her arm around her granddaughter. "It's not your fault." She paused. "But you should have called me."

Emily held her palm up. "I forgot my phone."

Charlotte sighed, wondering what to do next, but before she could come up with a plan, Bob said, "Come on in for a cup of coffee."

Kevin ran his hand over his closely cropped hair, looking a little befuddled. "Thank you."

"Char?" Bob glanced toward her.

"I'll start the coffee. You two can go sit in the living room." If Bob was feeling so amiable, then he could be the one to entertain their former son-in-law.

TEN MINUTES LATER, Christopher joined the grown-ups in the living room as they sipped their coffee.

"What have you been up to?" Bob asked Kevin.

"Working in Texas at a family-run manufacturing plant." He sat on the edge of the sofa. "The oil-rig work dried up, but I was happy for the other job—until I got laid off."

"And what brings you up this way?" Bob said.

"Well." Kevin folded his hands together. "I have a lead on a job in Harding. An old buddy told me about it."

"Where are you staying?" Bob asked.

"The Bedford Motel tonight." Kevin looked Bob in the eyes. "Then hopefully in Harding."

Charlotte cleared her throat, and both men and Christopher looked at her. She wanted to ask what his intentions were concerning the kids, but she couldn't do it in front of Christopher. "Sweetie," she said, "I forgot to check Toby's water this afternoon. It's so hot. Would you go fill it for me?"

He narrowed his eyes at her, obviously aware she was trying to get rid of him. "And grab a few cookies for yourself and your dad when you come back through the kitchen." She waited until she heard the back door bang and then said, "What are your plans as far as the kids?"

"What do you mean?"

"Why the job in Harding?"

He leaned back. "It's a job."

"And what does it mean for the kids?"

Kevin shook his head. "I'm not following you."

Charlotte tilted her head. Was he up to something?

"I think what Char is asking, is—" Bob took a deep breath. "How often do you want to see the kids, that sort of thing."

"Oh, now and then."

The back door banged again, and Charlotte heard

Christopher in the kitchen. Not surprisingly, Emily had shut herself in her bedroom.

Bob glanced at Charlotte and then back to Kevin. "How about if you come back for dinner tonight? Say around six thirty. You can see Sam then and spend more time with Emily and Christopher. That will give Char and me some time to talk."

"Okay." Kevin stood as Christopher came in with a handful of cookies and then offered half to Kevin. "Oh, no thanks," he said.

Christopher's face fell, but then Kevin rumpled his hair and he smiled a little. "I'll see you later tonight. Okay, squirt?"

"Ah, I wanted to show you my pumpkins."

"I could take time for that," Kevin said as the adults followed Christopher into the kitchen. Kevin told Charlotte and Bob good-bye and then followed Christopher outside.

"Go with them," Charlotte said.

Bob shook his head. "They're fine."

"Go with them or start dinner." Charlotte stood with her hands on her hips. "Pretend you're checking on the chickens or something. Just keep an eye on Christopher."

She wasn't ready to let the kids out of her sight.

Chapter Nine

Sam drummed his fingers against the computer table. Lyla was fifty minutes late. His phone beeped, and he wrestled it from his pocket, peering at the text. *Are you on your way home?* It was Emily. He thumbed in, *Not yet.*

Hurry, was her reply. Just as he started to respond, Lyla walked through the door. She looked like she was floating in some ghostly way or something, with her ankle-length skirt flowing around her and her long hair all wispy around her face.

She startled when she saw him and then smiled. "I forgot," she said. "Sorry." She dumped a stack of books on the table. "So do you want the job?"

"Sure," Sam answered.

"When can you start?"

"Tomorrow."

"Cool." She slid her backpack off her shoulder all the way down to the floor. "The first thing you'll need to do is update the website."

"Okay. What time will you be here?"

"I won't," she answered. "But I'll e-mail you all the copy."

"We'd better exchange info," Sam said, taking out his phone. She gave him her number and her e-mail address, and he did the same. "Any passwords on the computers?" Sam asked, trying to remember how she'd logged on the day before.

She shook her head. "I made Russell take all that stuff off."

"Do you have regular office hours?"

"Usually every afternoon, just not tomorrow." She settled down at the computer closest to her books. "Sometimes we have staff meetings, like today."

"Should I stick around?" Sam asked.

She flipped her hair over her shoulder. "There's no need."

"I'll see you day after tomorrow then," Sam said.

"Bye," she said, already absorbed in her e-mail.

As he drove home, Sam remembered Emily's last text. Grandma was adamant that he couldn't text and drive, or even talk on the phone and drive. He'd better not risk it. Grandma said she'd take his cell phone away if she caught him.

He turned up his music. Lyla was one of the more interesting girls he'd met at college so far. His friend Sally was great, but he wasn't sure where things stood with her exactly. Most of the other girls seemed high schoolish, self-conscious, and into their clothes and hair. Lyla seemed different. She also seemed older, maybe twenty or twenty-one. And she didn't seem to care at all what other people thought of her, especially Russell.

He hoped loading the stuff on the website wouldn't be too hard. He'd do some more research after dinner tonight; hopefully no one else would need the computer.

He glanced at the clock on his dashboard as he came up

behind a tractor poking along. Six o'clock. Hopefully he'd be home for dinner on time. He hated eating by himself. He'd call Uncle Bill tonight and ask if he could hold the job open for him for Christmas, spring, and summer vacations. Bill would understand.

Twenty-seven minutes later Sam turned into the driveway. Grandpa stood by the shed door, petting Toby. As Sam slowed, he started walking toward where Sam usually parked, near the oak tree. Grandpa waited with his arms crossed. "You're late."

"I got a job at the college." Sam climbed out of the car, realizing he'd forgotten to ask Lyla what the pay was. His face reddened at the realization, but Grandpa brought him back to the moment.

The old guy's voice was deeper than usual. "I need to talk with you."

Sam looked around. Had something happened? Were Emily and Christopher okay? He stuttered, "Ev- everyone all right?"

Grandpa nodded. "But your father stopped by today. And he's coming for dinner tonight."

"What?" Sam stepped back at Grandpa's bluntness, whacking his leg against the corner of his car door. As he bent down to rub his calf, a car turned into the driveway.

"That's him." Grandpa put his arm around Sam's shoulders and straightened him up. "He says he just wants to see all of you. That's all."

I'll bet. As Sam pulled away from Grandpa and retrieved his backpack from his car, his face began to grow even warmer. He had imagined sharing the news about his job during dinner and having everyone be proud of him. He turned and watched his father park an old junker of a car beside Grandma's and then climb from the front seat. His hair had some gray around the temples, and his forehead was wrinkly like he was worried about something. He wore jeans and an old shirt. He looked shorter than he had the last time. Sam expected him to pull bags of gifts out of the backseat, but he didn't.

Dad stepped toward Grandpa, his arm extended. "Bob," he said, shaking briskly. Then he turned toward Sam. "Son."

Sam took his hand. It was cold and clammy, and it shook slightly.

Sam opened his mouth but nothing came out.

"How's your car running?" his dad said, gesturing toward Sam's 240-Z.

"Fine." Sam kicked at a pebble.

"Let's go on in," Grandpa said. "Charlotte's dishing up."

Sam led the way. As he slipped into the kitchen Emily shot him a dirty look and hissed, "What took you so long?"

Christopher stepped close to him, and Grandma stopped dishing up the mashed potatoes. "Is he here?" she asked Sam.

"Yep."

Grandma rested the masher against the side of the pan. "Be polite," she whispered, just as Grandpa and Dad came through the back door.

"I already told him hello." Sam pushed Christopher forward.

Emily gave Sam another mean look and said, "We already saw him after school."

Grandma stepped back to the stove and finished dishing up the mashed potatoes; then she told everyone to wash up, that they would eat in a minute.

"Come on," Christopher said to his dad. "You can use the upstairs sink."

EMILY SAT BESIDE SAM, across from her father. She caught herself staring at him and looked away. He seemed more relaxed now than when they had seen him at Christmas. Grandma was prattling on about the other grandkids. "Dana, Pete's wife, is expecting next spring. So the kids will have another cousin nearby—actually right on the farm. Pete and Dana are in the middle of building a house near the property line."

"So the farm must be doing well?" Their dad phrased it as a question.

Emily cringed. Didn't he know it wasn't polite to ask questions like that?

"Well," Grandpa said, "I wouldn't say *well*. Farms are precarious businesses."

"Heather Creek Farm is doing just fine," Grandma said. She looked like she was about ready to kill Grandpa. As everyone sat silently, pretending to concentrate on the ham, potatoes, squash, sliced tomatoes, and green beans, Uncle Pete walked through the back door.

"Look who's here." Grandma's face looked like it was ready to crack.

"Kevin." Pete shoved his hands in his pockets.

Dad nodded but didn't say anything.

"Want to grab a plate?" Grandma asked.

"Nah. I told Dana I'd be home in a few minutes," Pete said, but he pulled a chair up beside Christopher and leaned forward. "Kevin, where are you living these days?"

"I've been in Texas, but I'm on my way to see a buddy in Harding about a job."

Emily could practically hear Pete suck in his breath. She didn't want her dad to move to Harding.

Pete acted as if he hadn't heard anything about a job. "The weather here is a little different than in Texas; that's for sure."

Dad smiled. "Well, Texas had its share of hurricane warnings. San Diego had the best weather." He paused a second and then said, "Do you miss it, kids?" He looked around the table.

Emily dropped her gaze, not wanting to meet his eyes. What did he think? Of course they missed San Diego. Mostly they missed their mom, but it wasn't like they thought about it every second of every minute of every day like they used to. Until he came around.

Christopher cleared his throat. "I like the snow. Last year I built an igloo that was pretty cool. And I can hit the barn with a snowball from the yard—at least I could last year."

"Driving in the snow is a lot of fun." Sam took another bite of mashed potatoes.

Grandma gave Sam one of those looks.

"Well, I'd better get going." Uncle Pete pushed his chair back and stood. "Bye all," he called over his shoulder as he headed toward the back door. Then he stopped and turned back. "Mom, we have an appointment Friday morning in Grand Island."

Grandma nodded her head.

"An appointment about what?" Grandpa asked.

"Oh, we're just completing some paperwork."

"On?" Grandpa looked at Pete.

"We'll talk later," Grandma said in her firmest voice.

Uncle Pete said, "Kevin, if I don't see you again, good luck."

"Oh, I'll be around."

Emily narrowed her eyes, wondering exactly what that meant.

"Okay, see you sometime then." Uncle Pete's voice didn't sound very hospitable, and a moment later the back door slammed.

"Pete was about Christopher's age when I first met him," Dad said.

"I know," Emily answered and then blushed. She almost said she'd read it in Mom's diary, but it would be stupid to bring that up.

Grandma stood and started clearing away plates. "I have apple pie for dessert."

"Sounds good," Kevin said, pushing back from the table. "I remember how delicious your pies are."

Emily picked up her plate and Sam's and followed Grandma into the kitchen. She wanted to groan out loud or cry or scream.

Grandma must have known she was upset because she patted her shoulder and whispered, "We'll talk later, okay?"

Emily nodded, trying to look calm, but inside her stomach twisted into knots.

CHRISTOPHER STOOD in front of Grandpa as Dad opened the door to his car. "I'll call in a day or two. Maybe it will be cooler and we can all go to the park. We can kick a soccer ball around or something." He looked straight at Sam.

"I'll probably have homework—or work."

"Oh." Dad sat down in his car but left the door open. "Well, I'll call. We can decide what to do then."

Christopher kicked at the gravel in the driveway and then glanced up. "Bye." He didn't say it very loudly.

"See you soon," Dad said, pulling his door shut. Everyone else said good-bye and then waved as he backed out and then rolled down the car window. "Good to see all of you," he called out.

Everyone except Emily waved again. She headed back to the house.

"Well, that was awkward," Sam said.

"It wasn't too bad," Grandma said, ruffling Christopher's hair, but it sounded like she was trying to be positive.

Christopher leaned against Grandma and sighed. It was weird how their dad had bought them all those presents last time. Christopher was glad he didn't do that again. Not that he didn't like getting gifts—it was just strange to get them from someone who hadn't been around for so long.

Grandma stepped away from Christopher and headed toward the house. "Did you finish your homework?"

Christopher shook his head. "I need to work on my project." He had a medieval history report due next week. He was researching medical practices.

Mostly what he was learning was that death carts were pretty busy during the Middle Ages. People died from all sorts of things—skin diseases, not eating enough fruits and vegetables, cuts, bad sanitation, pneumonia, leprosy. And lots of mothers and babies died too. Christopher followed Grandma into the house. The most disturbing thing he learned was that caesarean sections were done without any anesthetics or antibiotics during medieval times. Christopher grabbed his backpack on the way into the kitchen and then slid onto a dining room chair. "Grandma," he said, "will Dana have to have a C-section?"

Grandma turned toward him abruptly. "Why do you ask?"

"I came across some info for my medieval report."

"Well, if she does, we can be thankful that medical practices have advanced since then." She chuckled. "Most of us would be dead if we lived back then."

Christopher nodded.

"The strep infection Emily and Pete had last spring could have killed them back then. Grandpa's diabetes would have done him in. I probably would have died in childbirth with your mom."

"But my mom would be alive." Christopher stared at his notebook, and Grandma stepped closer. "You know, 'cause no cars back then."

Grandma sat down beside him and ruffled his hair again.

"I wish she was still here," Christopher said.

"I know," Grandma said.

"Especially when Dad shows up."

"Why's that?" Grandma's voice was soft and slow.

Christopher shrugged. "He just really makes me miss her."

"Me too," Grandma said, hugging him. "Me too."

Chapter Ten

Emily sat at Ashley's desk, flicking the beaded fringe of her purple lamp shade while Ashley laced up her boots.

"We should get going," Emily said. She hated to be late, even if it was just for the high school open house. She and Ashley were going to lead tours for the freshman parents. It was a little hokey. It wasn't like anyone who lived in Bedford didn't already know every nook and cranny of the high school. In fact most of the parents had probably attended school in the building.

Ashley grabbed her sweater off her bed. "Mom might let me borrow the car. Or we could walk."

"Let's drive. Definitely." Emily stood and picked up her book bag. She'd come to Ashley's after school. Grandma was going to meet her at the school—not that Grandma needed a tour, but she would go around and check in with Emily's teachers and then give Emily a ride home.

As Emily followed Ashley down the stairs, Ashley's cell started to ring. She pulled it from her pocket as they reached the bottom step. "It's Isabella," she said, answering it.

Emily stepped toward the door. Isabella seemed to have some sort of built-in timer.

"We were just leaving," Ashley said. "We're driving." There was a pause and then she said, "They could probably use another tour guide. Do you want a ride?"

Emily wrinkled her nose. Leave it to Ashley to be so gracious. She wished she had said she wanted to walk.

"Isabella's going to meet us there," Ashley said as she stuffed her phone back into her pocket.

"I heard."

"She didn't want to stay home by herself."

Emily cocked her head. Isabella had come to school that day and was her usual boisterous self.

"Her mom's at work. She's a nurse at the hospital in Harding."

"And her dad?" Emily asked.

Ashley exhaled slowly. "I'm not sure exactly. But I don't think he's home."

"Is he in jail?"

Ashley shrugged. "I don't know. I haven't asked." She turned toward the kitchen. "Mom, we're leaving."

Melody came through the door, a dishtowel over her shoulder. "Have fun. I'll come with Dad after he gets home."

Ashley hugged her mom and kissed her cheek.

"Thank you for dinner, Mrs. Givens," Emily said. "The fettuccine was delicious."

"You're welcome." Ashley's mom reached out and gave Emily a hug. "Come back soon."

Emily nodded. She loved Ashley's house. It was so warm and cozy, and her parents were the best.

"Emily." Ashley's mom seemed unusually hesitant. "Could I talk with you for just a moment before you leave?"

Emily nodded and followed Melody into the kitchen, feeling a little numb, wondering if she'd done something wrong. "I saw your dad yesterday," Melody said, leaning against the counter. "He came into the café."

Emily's face grew warm, and she couldn't seem to speak.

"We spoke a little. He said he saw you the night before."

Emily nodded. Yesterday she'd kept wondering if he was just going to show up again, and today it had been such a relief to be with Ashley.

"I didn't say much to him—didn't mention the open house at school or anything—but then I got to thinking that maybe you had invited him or maybe your grandmother had."

Emily shook her head as her throat tightened. "No. We didn't mention it to him." At least she hadn't.

"I just wondered." Melody's eyes were kind. She paused and then asked, "Are you okay?"

Emily nodded and stepped toward the door but then stopped. "Does Ashley know?"

"Know?"

"That my dad is around?"

Melody shook her head. "But a lot of people saw him at the café, and he said if he didn't get the job in Harding he would look for one in Bedford."

"Oh."

"So more people might know." Melody touched Emily's shoulder. "You can talk to Ashley about it, you know. She wouldn't share what you tell her with anyone else."

Emily knew Melody was right. She saw the way Ashley was with Isabella: protective and caring. Benevolent. But Emily didn't want to talk to her friend about her father. She didn't want Ashley to feel sorry for her, to treat her in a fragile way, the way she'd been treating Isabella. "Thank you, Mrs. Givens," Emily said.

She followed Ashley out to the car. What if her dad was at the school tonight? What if he read about the open house in the paper or someone had mentioned it to him? What if he just showed up?

EMILY FOLLOWED ASHLEY and Isabella up the concrete steps of the school. Isabella had met them in the parking lot and then began prattling on about an old romcom movie she had watched last night when she couldn't sleep, but she stopped talking as she led the way through the door.

A group of students milled around in the foyer, which smelled like fresh floor wax. Mr. Santos the guidance counselor approached with flyers and began giving everyone directions on conducting the tours. Each group would have two guides. Isabella grabbed Ashley's arm before Emily had a chance to catch her friend's eye. Everyone paired up quickly, and Emily was left without a partner. "We'll have three in our group," Ashley whispered. Emily sighed, wishing Isabella hadn't tagged along.

As Mr. Santos continued talking, Aunt Dana came through the front door with a stack of papers in her arms. "Emily," she said, "would you help me please?"

"Um, sure." Emily stepped toward her.

"Can you go out to my car and grab the box out of the back? It's unlocked. I have some more curriculum handouts for the parents; I took them home to collate last night."

Five minutes later, Emily bumped through the English room door with the box. Aunt Dana had the other handouts spread out on a table, and Emily staggered over with the box. "There's more than paper in here," she said, scooting the box onto the table.

"There are books on the bottom. Pete told me not to carry it in; he thought it was too heavy for me." Dana smiled. "He carried it to the car."

Emily lifted out the papers and then a complete collection of Shakespeare that was bigger than the San Diego phone book.

"Is your grandma coming?" Dana asked.

"Yep," Emily said.

"Well, she certainly has years and years of Bedford High School open houses under her belt."

Emily smiled. "I told her she didn't need to."

"But she insisted, right?"

Emily nodded.

"Of course." Dana smiled again, but then her face grew serious. "How about your father? Pete said he's in town."

Emily stepped back and crossed her arms. What was with everyone? Just because her dad stopped by for dinner two nights ago didn't mean he was involved in her life. "No."

As the word flew out, someone called out her name. "Are you helping us or not?" It was Isabella, standing in the doorway with Ashley beside her. "We're next up to lead a tour group."

"Already?"

"Let's go," Isabella boomed. "The freshman parents are out in droves."

Emily waved good-bye to Dana and followed her friends, wondering if they had overheard her conversation. Ashley had her usual sympathetic look on her face so it was hard to tell.

"Boy, Mrs. Stevenson is looking a little frumpy, isn't she?" Isabella said as they hurried down the hall.

"Excuse me?" Emily bristled.

"I know she's your aunt and all, but still, it's like she's letting herself go since she got married. Her hair looks all limp, and she has bags under her eyes."

"I've heard the start of the school year can be really hard on teachers," Ashley said. "And she's been sick—right, Em?"

"Right," Emily said, slowing down, letting the other girls pull ahead. She could only imagine what Isabella would say about her father. Emily shivered, even though the building was hot and stuffy.

THEY TOOK TWO GROUPS of parents through the high school, showing them the gym, the choir room, the auditorium with its new stage curtain, the library with the four new computers that everyone was so proud of, and the home-ec room with the new stove. The cooking class had made lemon bars, snickerdoodles, and brownies. That was everyone's favorite stop, and thankfully they had saved it for last; that had been Ashley's idea.

Isabella did most of the talking. She seemed to thrive on attention, and her voice grew louder with each stop. Each time they stopped in the choir room, Isabella would sing the scales as if she were an up-and-coming opera star. Emily stood at the back of the room and then slipped back into the hall. A second later, Ashley came out. "What's up?"

"I can't take her anymore."

"Her?"

"Isabella. She's really getting on my nerves."

Ashley crossed her arms. "Come on, she's having a really hard time right now."

Emily pursed her lips.

Ashley bumped against her and smiled. "Try to be benevolent, okay? She'll be better soon."

Emily bumped her friend back. "I'll try," she said, even though she had no intention of doing so. She might be able to tolerate the girl if she tried really hard, but benevolence was out of the question. Why did Ashley have to be so nice?

After the last tour, Emily decided to look around for Grandma, and she snuck away from Ashley and Isabella. She checked in her advanced-algebra classroom, but Grandma wasn't there. Then she went to her fourth-period history classroom. Ashley's parents were there talking with Mrs. Lorenz, the teacher, but Grandma wasn't in sight. Next she peeked into Aunt Dana's classroom. A woman with dark short hair was standing at the front of the classroom, and Dana had her arm around her. Emily stopped in the doorway.

"We really wanted the house," the woman said. "I'm so sorry."

"Don't worry about it," Dana said. "I'm just concerned about you and Isabella—and your husband."

"He's lost his job. He was a truck driver. And the lawyer we hired is expensive."

Dana patted the woman's back.

"He had a drinking problem a few years ago but was in recovery and was doing great. I can't believe this has happened." She shuddered. "At least the lady he hit is going to be okay. I don't know what we would do if anything really bad had happened." The woman took a raggedy breath. "I was supposed to go in to work at seven tonight, but I got someone to cover for me until ten. I really wanted to touch base with you—"

Emily stepped away from the doorway.

"Emily!" Ashley's voice echoed down the hall. Emily spun around. "There you are." Ashley and Isabella were headed toward her.

"I was looking for Grandma, but she's not in there." Emily hurried toward the two other girls. "Come on!"

"She's in the library," Isabella said. "Talking to Mr. Duncan."

"Is anyone with her?" Emily whispered to Ashley.

"Like . . . ?"

"Grandpa?" Emily's voice quivered.

Ashley had a puzzled look on her face. "I think she's by herself," she whispered back.

When they reached the library, Emily glanced around nervously. Mr. and Mrs. Givens were looking at a shelf of new books, and Hunter's father, Mr. Norris, was talking with Grandma. Emily exhaled.

"Are you about ready to go?" Grandma asked.

"Have you checked in with all my teachers?"

"They all said you're off to a good start," Grandma said. "Except Dana. She was busy when I stopped in. I didn't disturb her."

As Emily stole a glance at Isabella, the girl's mother walked into the library, followed by Aunt Dana.

"Oh, there you are." Isabella's mother approached her. It was obvious that the woman had been crying. "I was just talking to Mrs. Stevenson."

A look of horror passed over Isabella's face, and then she said quietly, "I thought you were at work."

"I don't have to go in until ten."

"Oh." Isabella hooked elbows with her mom and directed her out the door.

"Bye," Ashley called out. "See you tomorrow."

Isabella waved her hand over her head as she turned into the hall.

"Everything okay?" Grandma asked Dana.

Aunt Dana nodded but didn't say anything.

Grandma seemed a little flustered, as if she regretted butting in. Then she added, as if it were an afterthought, "With Emily. In your class?"

"Oh." Aunt Dana seemed relieved. "Of course. She's doing fine. We're reading *To Kill a Mockingbird*."

Grandma nodded.

"Emily had some good things to say about the book the other day during class discussion. It's a good class."

Emily wandered over to Ashley as Grandma and Aunt Dana kept talking. "What's up with Isabella?" she asked.

Ashley shrugged. "She's embarrassed; that's all."

In a few minutes Ashley left with her parents, Hunter,

who had been leading tours too, came looking for his dad. Grandma hugged Aunt Dana good-bye, and she and Emily left the school, stepping out into the warm evening. The sky was studded with stars.

As they climbed into the car, Emily asked if her dad had stopped by or called.

"No," Grandma answered, fastening her seat belt.

"I was afraid maybe he would come to the open house."

"Afraid?" Grandma started the car.

"I would have been mortified."

Grandma pulled out of the parking lot. "I didn't even think to tell him about the open house."

Emily groaned.

"And if I *had* thought of it, I wouldn't have, Emily."

"Really?" Emily sat up straight.

"There's no reason for him to come." Grandma looked straight ahead as she drove, intent on the beam of the headlights in front of them.

For the first time Emily wondered what it was like for Grandma to have Kevin Slater show up out of the blue.

"You shouldn't be ashamed of your father or embarrassed," Grandma said. "His decisions and actions are his own. But he hasn't invested in your education. There would be no reason for him to meet your teachers." Grandma smiled at her quickly and then fixed her eyes back on the road.

"But what if he had shown up? How would I introduce him?" Emily clasped her hands together.

"As your father." Grandma reached over and placed her hand on top of Emily's.

Chapter Eleven

Pete climbed out of the backseat of his dad's pickup, feeling like a kid in a whole lot of trouble. No one had said a word the whole way to Grand Island.

Dad opened the door of the Great Plains State Bank main branch, and Mom walked through. Then Dad put out his foot, stopping Pete. "Let me do the talking," he said.

Pete took off his hat and nodded.

Mom had spilled the beans to Dad the night before about the loan, and Dad had torn their files apart, looking for the documentation. Pete had looked at home, thinking the file might have gotten in with some of his papers, but he couldn't find it.

A minute later they were sitting in a cubicle with a loan officer who hardly looked up from his computer screen. Dad spread the letter and the statement that had come in the mail on the desk. "We negotiated a non-real-estate farm loan—like we have many other times with your organization. And then we got a notice that we have a balloon payment due for ten thousand dollars."

The man punched in some numbers. "Yes, that's right. On a twenty-year loan."

"No," Dad said. "This was a short-term loan." He turned to Pete. "How many months?"

"Six."

The man shook his head. "Nope, this is a twenty-year loan."

Dad inhaled deeply and exhaled. The man finally looked up from his computer.

"There's been a mistake," Dad said. "I paid off a twenty-year loan—and yes, it had a ten-thousand-dollar balloon payment five years ago. There's a mistake in your records."

Pete didn't remember a twenty-year loan from before, but that was before his parents had included him in the farm's finances. He leaned back in the chair, bumping it against the partition. Honestly, it was a relief to have Dad involved. He should have told him sooner.

The loan officer shook his head. "I don't think there's been a mistake, but if you show me your documentation I can compare it to ours. Did you bring it with you?"

Dad stood. "We'll fax it over." He grabbed the man's card from the corner of his desk. "And I need the name of your supervisor."

The officer gave Dad a name and stood, extending his hand. "Nice to meet you. I'm sure we'll get this ironed out in no time."

"I'm sure you will," Dad said.

Mom led the way out of the bank, followed by Dad. Pete tagged along behind, dreading the ride back home.

THAT AFTERNOON, Pete stopped at the edge of the field and pulled his hat from his head, wiping his brow with the sleeve of his denim shirt, feeling better. He was a farmer, not a businessman. He squinted upward. But he knew he couldn't run the farm with that kind of attitude.

The sun was high and hot, really hot. He started down the row between the plants, scanning the leaves as he walked along. The soil was dry and powdery. He squinted against the noon sun. So far no spots. Maybe the fungus had been contained in the low field.

Halfway toward the creek he stopped and bent down, one knee in the dirt. At first he thought he was seeing things, but as he took the leaf in his hand he knew he wasn't. It was the fungus. Another plant, a few yards farther along, had several leaves that were infected too. Then there was nothing until he reached the end of the field just above the creek.

Still, it wasn't bad. He hoped the forecast for more rain was wrong. He rolled a spotted leaf between his hands as he headed toward his truck. The stems of the plants looked okay, and so did the seed pods. If someone was sabotaging the crops, it was more likely that the fields closest to the road would be infected, not those near the creek.

He hopped into his truck, deciding to head down to Frank's place to powwow with him and try to figure out how to put an end to the fungus. He couldn't imagine going plant by plant and pulling off the leaves. He didn't have time to do that.

He pulled onto the highway and accelerated. An old beater was headed his way. Pete squinted as the sun shone off the asphalt. It was Kevin's car. Sure enough, Kevin waved as he sped by. Maybe he was headed back out to the farm.

In a minute, just before Pete reached Frank's driveway, a truck from Brask Farms sped by. Pete slowed and watched it in his rearview mirror. Maybe the driver was headed up to the grain elevator to check on the numbers. He tried to remember if the operation had a parcel of land out that way, but he couldn't remember that either. He would ask his dad.

Pete turned slowly. Frank's truck was parked by his shop, and Pete pulled up beside it. As he slammed his door, Frank appeared, wiping his hands on a faded red rag.

"Howdy," Frank called out.

Pete nodded, stuffing his hands into his pockets. "Hey, I wanted to check in about the fungus." He'd already called all the neighbors to let them know it was a mutation. "I'm thinking it's not that big of a deal. The weather report says the storms are supposed to ease off, so I'm thinking we're out of the woods."

Frank was shaking his head before Pete stopped talking. "I have more, a lot more. Especially down by the creek. And so does Silas."

"Really?" Pete pulled his hat off his head and ran his hand through his hair.

Frank was smiling now. "Silas is sure it's a diabolical plot to get his farm. Says he's seen a corporate farmhand down by the creek several times late at night."

Pete rubbed the side of his face. "Not to raise any alarms or anything, but a Brask Farms truck just drove by." He smiled at his attempt to make a joke, but Frank kept a straight face. "What are you going to do?" Pete asked. "About the fungus."

Frank shrugged. "There's no pesticide, right?"

"Correct," Pete said.

"Do you think it's going to affect our yield?"

Pete shrugged his shoulders. "At this point, it depends on how things go. If the plants get too stressed the beans won't mature."

Frank wiped the back of his neck with the rag and then swatted at a fly. "I guess I'll give it a few more days before I start to worry."

"Sounds like a plan," Pete said, stepping back toward his pickup.

"Say, how's that house of yours coming along?"

"The new one?"

Frank nodded.

"Things are stalled right now," Pete said.

"Hannah said your house in town sold."

Pete winced. Obviously the grapevine was breaking down. "We thought it did, but the buyer backed out."

"That's a shame." Frank's blue eyes showed empathy. "These are uncertain times; that's for sure."

Pete nodded, scanning the horizon. And Frank had no idea what stress they were under—not just because of the house deal falling through but also because of the loan mix-up. The beginning of a thundercloud billowed in the distance, and the afternoon was growing muggy. "Well, I'd better get back to work," Pete said.

"Take it easy in this heat," Frank flung the rag over his shoulder. "Maybe you can find some inside work to do."

Pete shook his head. "Not today. I'm off to check the corn—to make sure some weird blight hasn't developed." He tried to smile.

Frank waved as he turned back toward his shop.

Pete was sure the corn crop was fine. He just didn't want to miss anything.

LATE IN THE AFTERNOON, Pete parked his pickup in front of his and Dana's new house. He stepped to the ground, stretched, yawned, and then walked through the framed garage into the kitchen, breathing in the warm scent of the pine lumber. The interior walls would go up once they had more money. The plan was that Pete would do the finishing work, the trim work and painting during December and January. Then they would move in by February. The house in town had to sell so they could pay the contractor, the plumber, the electrician, and the drywaller.

His boots echoed across the cement floor. He turned around slowly in the living room. The couch would go under the window, the piano along the far wall. Pete was negotiating to have the TV in the living room in one of those fancy cabinets—if they could afford it. Otherwise Dana wanted it in the back bedroom that they would use as the den until they needed it as a bedroom. Dana wanted to have Grandma Maxie move in with them someday if she needed to.

He started up the staircase, aware of each step. He reached the second-floor landing and looked over the Freemans' cornfield; then he headed to the baby's room, stopping at the framed-in window that faced Heather Creek. He shivered even though the afternoon had grown downright steamy. The entire sky was filled with storm clouds now, and the branches of the willow trees along the creek swayed in the sticky breeze.

He hoped his child—daughter or son—would love the creek as much as he did. He used to play cowboy and cavalry and pioneer days along the creek, running up and down the banks, climbing the trees, catching frogs and minnows and salamanders in the shallow water and mud. Pete smiled. He would be able to do all of that again, with a good excuse. And Christopher would be there with them, enjoying every minute. What a fortunate kid his and Dana's baby was going to be.

He heard the engine of a car approaching, and then it

stopped. He hoped it wasn't his dad. The last thing he needed was a reminder about how he was mismanaging the farm or how bad their finances were or how foolish he'd been to think he could build a house on the land.

He moved toward the staircase.

"Pete?" It was Dana's voice.

"Up here," he called back, thumping down the stairs.

"There you are." She stood in the middle of their future living room, looking beautiful with her hair half undone and hanging loosely around her head. She wore a short-sleeved shirt that pulled a little against her belly, a blue skirt, and low-heeled sandals. She had dark circles under her eyes, but she was still gorgeous. He bent to hug her.

"I decided to leave school at a decent time and come see the house. It was nice to see your pickup already parked here."

"This is the first time I've stopped by all week." He reached for her hand. "Come up and see the baby's room."

He led her to the stairs, hanging onto her hand as they took the steps one at a time. She smiled as he pulled her into the nursery. "Look at the view," he said. "We can put the rocking chair right by the window."

Dana let go of his hand and took another step. "It's beautiful," she said.

Pete stood behind her, wrapping his arms around her, saying nothing. The house was modest—three bedrooms and two baths. There was a little office area off the kitchen and a basement they could finish later, perhaps make into a family room in the next few years.

Dana startled at a crack of thunder in the distance.

Pete groaned. Another round of thunder crashed all around them.

"Does this place have a lightning rod on it yet?" Dana joked as the torrential rain began.

Pete shook his head. "Probably not."

Another round of thunder shook the structure. "We might as well wait for the rain to slow," Pete said, pulling Dana down to the floor. They leaned their backs against the inside wall studs.

"How do you like your house, Mrs. Stevenson?" Pete joked.

"It's lovely, Mr. Stevenson," Dana answered, cuddling closer. "I just hope we can pay for it."

"Shhh," he said. "Don't think about that now." He kissed her perky nose.

"Maybe things will work out with Isabella's family." Dana sighed. "I don't know of anyone else in Bedford who is looking for a house right now."

"Her dad would have to find a job in Bedford though, and I don't know of anyone who's hiring." Pete didn't want to think about their house in town or the buyers who had backed out. Or the farm loan. He hadn't told Dana about that; he didn't want her to have another thing to worry about.

"Uncle Pete!"

Pete smiled. Saved by Christopher.

"Are you in here?"

"Up here," Pete said. "Careful on the stairs."

Christopher's blond head appeared. "I was playing down at the creek." The rain had soaked through his T-shirt and jeans. "Can you believe this rain?" He collapsed at the top of the stairs. "I thought I was going to drown."

"You and the soybean plants," Pete said, offering Christopher his hand.

Chapter Twelve

Charlotte followed Hannah across the creek on the wooden bridge on Sunday afternoon, swatting at mosquitoes as she hurried along. She'd forgotten to put on repellent before she left to meet her friend. She buttoned the top of her shirt and rolled down the sleeves.

"Don't the mosquitoes seem to be hanging around later this year?" Charlotte buttoned her cuffs, one after the other.

"It's all the rain we keep having. Storm after storm. And all this humidity—it's worse than normal too. You'd think we lived in the tropics."

Charlotte agreed. The path widened, and she increased her stride, catching up to her friend. "Let's head back to the road. This is ridiculous." She swatted at a mosquito that was buzzing around her face. The women turned around and hurried back across, aiming downstream for the Carters' property and then along the edge of their cornfield to their driveway and back toward the road.

"Has Bob set a retirement date yet?" Hannah asked.

"No, he's having a hard time making that decision." She could say that much without going into all the details about the loan being a major setback in Bob's being willing to turn the farm over to Pete. He had been livid on Friday and absolutely silent since.

"That's a hard one," Hannah said. "And it's a problem we won't ever have." She sighed. "Maybe Pete can buy our land when we're ready to retire and move into town."

Charlotte smiled, wondering if her friend was thinking about Frank's recent heart attack and how close she had come to losing him.

"Or lease it," Hannah added.

Heather Creek Farm would have to be bringing in a lot more revenue than it was right now for Pete to buy or even lease additional land. "That's an idea. Or you could sell to the corporate farm like the Millers and Westmorelands did." Charlotte was half serious. If she were in Hannah and Frank's shoes, she'd be tempted.

"No, thank you," Hannah said. "I'd rather leave the land to Pete."

Charlotte didn't respond. Hannah and Frank would need the money for their golden years. She'd read recently that a third of all farmland in the U.S. was owned by people over sixty-five. If those seniors didn't have children who wanted to farm, chances were the land would be sold to a corporation; but she understood Hannah's hesitation. She couldn't bear the thought of having Heather Creek Farm absorbed, the house and barn abandoned.

She shivered even as sweat ran down the back of her neck. She was so thankful that she and Bob had Pete and that he wanted to farm more than anything. "What project are you working on right now?" she asked Hannah, attempting again to change the subject.

"I started crocheting a baby blanket for Dana and Pete's baby—yellow and green with little frogs around the edges."

Charlotte's heart swelled. Hannah was the best. Pete had

told Hannah by accident the other day when he'd stopped by to see Frank. She'd promised not to tell anyone else. They reached the road and started along the gravel shoulder.

"Just think: we'll have a shower for Dana soon." Hannah's blue eyes lit up. "I can't wait. I'm so excited about this baby."

"Me too," Charlotte said, swallowing a lump in her throat. "Bonnie Simons thought I wouldn't be since it's my seventh grandchild, but—I can't explain it—each baby is such a gift. I couldn't be any more excited if it were my first."

"Has Kevin come by again?" Hannah increased her pace as they crested the hill toward Heather Creek Farm.

"No. He called yesterday and said he'd stop by in a day or two." Charlotte had been trying not to anticipate the worst. She'd gone from worrying about the bank loan to fretting about Kevin and whether he planned to seek custody of the children.

"I thought maybe he'd left," Hannah said.

"I was beginning to think that too."

"Hoping, right?"

Charlotte paused. "Yes. And no. Honestly, I don't know what to hope. So far the kids don't seem too upset by his visit, but having him still in the area and not knowing what his plans are is unnerving—at least for me. I can't imagine what it's like for the kids."

"Are you going to talk to the lawyer again?"

"Probably." Charlotte wasn't sure what to do. It all depended on what Kevin did next.

Ahead, a car turned onto Heather Creek Lane.

"You have company," Hannah said as Charlotte increased her pace.

"It's Kevin." Charlotte started to jog. "Let's hurry."

EMILY PULLED THE CURTAIN back from her window. Her dad's car was coming up the driveway, and Christopher was running toward it. She rammed the heels of her hands against the sash of the window, opening it all the way and sticking her head out, looking for Grandma. She'd gone walking with Hannah a half hour ago. Emily squinted against the afternoon sunshine. In the distance, on the shoulder of the highway, she saw two figures moving toward the farm.

Emily shoved her window shut and hurried down the stairs. "Hey," she called out to Sam, who was sitting in a daze in front of the computer, "Dad just turned into the driveway."

"So?" He didn't even turn around.

"Christopher's out there by himself."

Sam shrugged.

Emily groaned and kept going, her ponytail bouncing against her neck. Christopher shouldn't be alone with their father. Who knew what he might say to him or try to talk him into? She banged through the back door and stepped out onto the lawn into the bright sunshine. Dad's hand rested on Christopher's shoulder. When he saw Emily he stepped away.

"I stopped by to see if you three kids wanted to go into town for ice cream."

"We're working on homework," Emily answered, stopping beside her little brother.

"I'm all done," Christopher said, turning his head toward her.

"Well, Grandma isn't here."

"We can ask Grandpa."

"He's napping," Emily said, just as their grandfather came out of the shed.

"Hello," Grandpa said to Dad, hooking his thumbs into his suspenders as he walked.

"I *thought* he was napping," Emily muttered.

Dad stepped forward and shook Grandpa's hand. "I was just asking the kids if they wanted to get ice cream."

"Is that right?" Grandpa stood with his feet apart and his thumbs still stuck in his suspenders. It was funny how, even though he was old, he looked a lot stronger, a lot scarier, than her father or any other man Emily knew. Not scary in a bad way, not like he would hurt anyone, but like he wasn't someone you wanted to mess with, ever.

Dad nodded but didn't say anything.

"What have you been up to?" Grandpa asked.

"I've been staying with my buddy in Harding—not at the motel in Bedford. That's why I haven't come by."

Emily frowned. That would have been nice to know Thursday night when she was terrified that he was going to show up at the school.

"My friend works at a manufacturing plant outside of Harding, just off the highway. I have an interview there first thing tomorrow." Dad looked proud of himself, standing up straight, a smile on his face.

"Is that right?" Grandpa said again. Emily's stomach lurched.

Dad nodded as his smile faded. "I've been applying everywhere I can think of." He looked dejected.

"Here comes Grandma," Christopher said, pointing toward the windbreak. Sure enough, Grandma and Hannah were racewalking toward them, their faces flushed, their arms pumping up and down.

"Looks like you two have had quite a workout," Grandpa said and then chuckled.

Grandma was so out of breath she couldn't talk when she reached them. Sweat beaded along her forehead, and her graying hair was moist and pushed back. Sweat spots dotted Hannah's faded T-shirt like sporadic puddles under a row of ducks parading across her chest.

Hannah waved her hand at Kevin instead of speaking.

"Do you remember our neighbor, Hannah Carter?" Grandpa said.

Dad reached out his hand and said, "Pleased to meet you."

Hannah wiped her hand on her jeans before taking his. "The same," she managed to say.

"Kevin wants to take the kids into town for ice cream," Grandpa said.

"But we have homework," Emily added.

Christopher shook his head. "I don't."

"Well, Sam and I do."

"I guess it's just you and me, buddy," Dad said.

Emily felt a wave of panic and looked at Grandma. "Go ask Sam," Grandma said. "Maybe he's done." Grandma's face was pale, and beads of sweat had collected above her upper lip.

Emily turned toward the house. Why didn't Grandma just say Christopher couldn't go? She looked like she wanted to.

"Sam," she called out, banging through the back door. "You're going into town for ice cream. With Dad and Christopher."

"'Fraid not," Sam said. "I have to finish this essay."

"Then he's taking Christopher by himself."

"So?" Sam spun around in the computer chair.

"So! Do you want Christopher alone with Dad?"

Sam shrugged.

"Listen, Sam Slater, just because you're old enough that you can choose where you live doesn't mean that Dad wouldn't try to make Christopher live—"

"What are you talking about?"

"Dad. Custody. Christopher."

"You're crazy. Grandma and Grandpa would never let that happen."

"What if they don't have a choice? Or what if he convinces Christopher to live with him?" Emily stepped closer to Sam. "He's getting a job in Harding."

"What?" Sam spun around.

"Come *on!*" Emily said.

"I'm not going for ice cream." Sam turned back to the computer.

"Then I'll go. I'm not letting Christopher go alone."

"Fine." Sam stared straight ahead.

Emily headed back outside, her feet stomping down the two steps to the yard.

"I'm coming," Emily called out, glaring at the faces in the semicircle ahead of her. Someone needed to act responsibly. Hopefully no one she knew would be at Jenny's Creamery on this particular Sunday afternoon. She patted the pocket of her jeans, even though she knew her cell phone was wedged inside. Grandma caught her eye and gave her a nod of approval.

EMILY TIPPED HER SPOON and stared at the chocolate syrup drizzling over the cherry on top of her sundae. She leaned back against the red vinyl of the booth.

"Tell me about your friends," Dad said to Christopher as

he tapped his foot on the black-and-white checked linoleum floor.

"Hmm," Christopher said. "I don't have many."

"Ah, come on." Dad had his hands wrapped around a cup of coffee that he hadn't even sipped. He smiled. "Then tell me about your enemies."

"That's easy. Justin Taylor. He picks on me all the time."

"How so?"

"Trash talk. Wet willies. Headlocks." Christopher shrugged as he took another bite of his strawberry sundae. "You know. That sort of thing."

Dad had an expression on his face like he did know.

"Christopher, you have friends," Emily said. "You have Dylan. And Wyatt." They were both geeks, but still, they were who he hung around with.

"Yeah. They're okay."

Emily leaned forward. "And Sam and me. And Uncle Pete. And Grandma and Grandpa."

"You guys are family," Christopher said.

"And friends." Emily looked straight at her father and then back at Christopher. "Aren't you lucky to have us be both?"

Christopher gave her a bewildered look, took another bite, and then addressed their father. "What happened to your cool red truck?"

"It was too expensive." Dad tightened his grip on his cup. "Between the payments and insurance, it took too much of my income. But it wasn't until I got laid off that I sold it."

"And bought that car?" Christopher nodded toward the parking lot.

"Yep."

"How come you got laid off?"

"Last hired, first fired."

Christopher's eyes grew wide. "You were fired?"

Dad chuckled. "Not really. Let go. First with the oil rig and then the plant."

"And now you're going to live in Harding?"

Dad finally took a sip of his coffee, swallowed, and then directed his gaze past Christopher. "Maybe."

The bell on the door of the creamery chimed. Emily stole a glance over the booth, hoping whoever just came in wouldn't recognize her. She tried not to react; it was Isabella's mom with a man. Probably her dad. Emily stared for a moment, expecting Isabella to come through the door too, but she didn't. She slumped back against the booth, expecting the couple to sit at one of the tables closer to the door. But a moment later, Isabella's mom was standing at their table.

"Emily? You're Isabella's friend, right?"

Emily nodded.

"I saw you at school the other night." She turned toward the man. "This is Izzy's father." The man had short blond hair and didn't look like someone with a drinking problem.

"Nice to meet you." Emily sat up straight.

Dad stood. "This is Emily's brother Christopher." Christopher smiled. "And I'm her father, Kevin. Kevin Slater." He smiled and extended his hand. "Would you like to join us?"

"Oh, thanks, but we don't want to intrude." Isabella's mom smiled and then said to Emily, "I asked Izzy to come with us, but she's feeling . . . self-conscious. She would have come if she'd known you were going to be here though. She's quite fond of you and—what's the other girl's name?"

"Ashley."

"That's right. Anyway, I'll make sure and tell Isabella I saw you."

"Thanks," Emily muttered as Mr. and Mrs. Dobbs headed to the other end of the creamery.

EMILY SAT AT HER PLACE at the dining room table, her arms crossed, her legs outstretched, and her eyes set in a glare.

"Em, did you hear me?" Grandma was leaning on the table.

"What?"

"Pardon me?"

"Whatever." Emily stood, picking up her plate and glass. Everyone else had left the table.

"How did it go, getting ice cream?"

"Fine." Emily put her dishes in the sink with a clatter and turned on the water to rinse them.

"Christopher said he had fun." Grandma was beside her now, rinsing her own plate.

"It's not all about fun, is it?" Emily lowered her plate into the dishwasher.

"What do you mean?" Grandma's voice was soft and low.

"I can't believe you just let Dad waltz in here. And you would have let Christopher go off to ice cream alone with him."

"Emily."

"He could have taken Christopher. Or talked him into moving in with him."

"Em, I really don't think—"

"You said the other night that you didn't think it was a good idea for Dad to come around."

"Sweetie, I don't, but I have no reason to forbid him from visiting."

"It's your property." Emily slammed the dishwasher door closed, but it bounced back and fell down again.

Grandma put her plate into the machine and then closed it carefully.

"If he said he was taking us to live with him, would you let him?"

"Of course not." Grandma put her arm around Emily. "There, there," she said.

"Why did he have to come around again?" Emily was crying now.

"Because he wants to see you."

"But he just makes it harder."

Grandma drew Emily closer, enveloping her in her arms.

"You know, in Mom's diary, when she wrote about Dad, when she first met him, he sounded so good. So decent."

Emily could feel Grandma's head nodding.

"Do you think he was?"

"I think he probably still is. He's made mistakes, Emily. Big mistakes. But he isn't all bad."

Emily thought of her dad standing to shake hands with Isabella's parents. He'd looked almost normal. He wanted to meet the parents of someone he thought was her friend.

But there was nothing normal about him.

"Why doesn't this bother the boys like it does me?" Emily asked.

"We don't know that it doesn't." Grandma stepped back and took Emily's face in her hands. "They might just show it differently."

"No. I can tell. It doesn't bother them at all."

"Emily."

"How can they forget what he did to Mom? To all of us? It's like they've forgiven him or something." Emily wiped her eyes with the sleeve of her T-shirt.

"Emily, if you don't forgive your dad, it's going to hurt you more than it will him."

Emily hated it when adults spoke that way. She wasn't going to forgive him for leaving. If he hadn't left maybe Mom would still be alive. She pulled away from Grandma, hurried up the stairs to her room, and burst into sobs as she flung herself across her bed.

CHARLOTTE FLUFFED HER PILLOW and then climbed under the sheet. "Bob?" she said. "Bob?"

He turned toward her, his eyes heavy.

"Have you forgiven Kevin?"

"For?"

"Leaving Denise and the children."

He propped his head on his hand. "I thought you meant for showing up again." He smiled.

"Have you?"

"Sure. That was a long time ago, right? It doesn't do any good not to forgive him." He scratched his chin. "Have you?"

"I don't trust him; that's for sure."

"Forgiveness and trusting aren't the same thing."

"I know." She turned off the bedside light and stared at the ceiling. "Emily hasn't forgiven him, and I wonder if I'm setting a bad example."

"How so?" Bob reached for her hand in the dark.

"By being negative."

"I've never heard you say anything negative about him." He grinned. "Not to the children anyway."

"I think Emily picks up on it anyway." Charlotte yawned. Denise had been that way too, able to discern what Charlotte was feeling without Charlotte verbally expressing her emotions.

"She and Christopher seem to have had a good time going into town with Kevin." Bob's voice was fading.

"Emily didn't. She was upset, even before they left."

"She shouldn't have gone then."

"She thought it was irresponsible of us to be ready to let Christopher go alone with Kevin." Charlotte turned her head toward Bob.

His eyes were closed, and he spoke slowly. "What did she think Kevin was going to do?"

Charlotte didn't answer, and in another minute Bob let out a snore. A slight breeze wafted through the lace curtain. She turned her face toward it. In the distance, thunder crashed again.

Kevin seemed down and out compared with the last time he'd come around, driving that big red truck and buying gifts. He probably didn't have enough money to set up a household of his own yet, even if he did get the job tomorrow. Then again, maybe his new humble-pie attitude was a ruse. Maybe he had something up his sleeve.

Even the trip to town for ice cream had a special appeal to Christopher; it really was a treat, not something they did very often. She couldn't compete with Kevin if he started trying to win Christopher's affection.

Thunder crashed again; then a streak of lightning flashed, followed by a clap directly overhead. Charlotte pulled the pillow over her head as the rain began to fall.

Chapter Thirteen

Monday afternoon, Sam stood in front of the door of the newspaper lab and tried the handle for the second time. It was definitely locked. He peered through the tinted narrow window into the dark room. He could make out the computer table but couldn't see Lyla. She'd said she was in every afternoon. He dug his cell phone from his pocket and dialed her number. She didn't answer, but a second after he hung up the phone vibrated.

"I missed your call." It was Lyla.

"I'm outside the lab, waiting for you."

"Use your key." She sounded tired.

"What key?" He slumped against the door.

"The key I gave you."

He didn't answer.

"Don't tell me I forgot."

"You forgot."

"Go to the secretary in the English department; she'll let you in. I'll be there in a half hour or so."

"Thanks," Sam muttered and hung up his phone, already on his way down the hall to the office.

Five minutes later he was sitting in front of one of the Macs. He was actually relieved not to have Lyla around. He was having a hard time figuring out the InDesign program used for the website and had Googled tutorials the evening before at home, but the Internet out at the farm was slow and kept crashing.

He Googled the subject again and then clicked onto a tutorial. A site popped up saying it took only three easy steps to create a website. That wasn't the problem. The site was already created; he needed to know how to change the content. He clicked onto the video anyway. Maybe once he knew how to get into the site he could archive the old content and add the new.

The door opened, and Sam turned toward it, expecting Lyla. Instead, Russell came into the room.

"Oh, hi," Russell said, pushing a strand of long hair behind his ear. "You took the job?"

Sam nodded.

"How's it going?"

"Okay." Sam minimized the tutorial. "What's up with you?"

"I e-mailed Lyla some questions but haven't heard back from her. I thought I'd try to talk to her in person."

"You write for the paper?"

"Nope. I sell ads. That's why I quit the computer tech stuff; it took too much time. Too many hours and not enough money."

"Oh." Sam turned his attention back to the computer and clicked onto his e-mail, where Lyla had forwarded the new content for the site.

"I've told Lyla over and over that maintaining the website is too much work, that the job is too hard." He flung his backpack onto the table. "So what do you think? How are things going with the site?"

"Fine," Sam muttered.

"Cool. Well." Russell unzipped his pack. "Let me know if you have questions. The whole design thing is my forte except that it's so time-consuming. I get paid whether I sell an ad or not, and selling takes a lot less time."

"Then why aren't you?" It was Lyla, coming through the door. She wore the same floaty skirt she had on last week, and her hair was all twisted on top of her head. "We could use the revenue."

"I need to talk with you about the prices."

"Prices?"

"I e-mailed you to say I thought they were too high. No one's buying."

"I haven't gotten any e-mails from you."

Sam scooted closer to the computer as the two kept bickering. Lyla said Russell should go get his hair cut because people in Nebraska liked conservative salespeople.

Russell stomped out of the room, and Lyla stomped into her office.

Sam went back to the tutorial and figured out how to get into the website. It took him another half hour to figure out how to post the stories from the last issue. Just as he hit PREVIEW the lights went off and the computer crashed.

"Hey!" Sam called out.

Lightning lit up the window.

"Another storm. Can you believe it?" Lyla stepped back into the main room.

Sam shook his head. "It's been crazy."

"But we've hardly gotten any rain. Hey, where do you live anyway?"

"Bedford. Actually on a farm near there."

"Bedford? Where's that?"

"Past Harding."

"Yikes. So you're a farm boy, huh?"

Sam nodded, thinking he needed to tell her he was really from San Diego, but she kept talking.

"Well, there's not much you can do until the electricity comes back on, but thankfully I printed off hard copies to edit." She started back to her office.

"Actually I have a couple of questions for you," Sam said.

She stopped and faced him. "Shoot."

"You didn't mention what the pay for the job was."

"You didn't ask." She crossed her arms.

"I'm asking now." His palms felt clammy.

"A stipend of five hundred dollars for the term."

Sam nodded. "Okay, thanks." He was hoping he would be paid by the hour, but still, he'd be able to cover almost all of his tuition this way.

Lyla exhaled and then said, "Russell didn't think it was enough. He said he put in way too many hours that spring term. He wanted full tuition this term and a bigger stipend. Like I had any say in it, but he thought I did. Thing was, he wasted a lot of time."

"Tuition? No one said anything about tuition."

Lyla cocked her head. "I'm sure I did."

"Nope."

"Oh." She shrugged. "Yeah. You get half tuition too."

Sam stood and lifted his backpack. "Cool." That would

help. He hadn't expected any breaks on his tuition. That would make Grandma happy. He hadn't paid his bill yet; he would do it tomorrow. Now he just needed to figure out the website.

"Russell wasted a ton of time." Lyla had a gift of picking up a thread of conversation from several minutes back. "It was unbelievable. And he was always griping." She threw up her arms.

"Well, I've got to go. I'll be back in tomorrow." Sam started to step backward.

"And to give him more money I would have had to take less." Lyla's face was flushed, and a strand of hair was hanging in her face.

"Go figure," Sam said, heading straight for the door. "I'll see you tomorrow." Last week he'd found Lyla attractive, but he wasn't so sure now. She seemed to be carrying a grudge against Russell. If Sam wanted to succeed at the job he was going to have to figure out how to stay on her good side.

As he walked down the stairs, he dialed Uncle Bill's law office. Surprisingly, Bill was able to take his call. When Sam told him he had a job at the college that was more convenient, Bill said he wasn't surprised.

"Could I work for you over vacations?" Sam asked.

"Most likely," Bill said. "Call the week before and double-check. We always have files piling up that need to be taken care of. I don't see that changing."

Sam thanked him sincerely and hung up. He *would* figure out the website. He didn't have any choice now.

It wasn't until he reached the parking lot that he realized

he hadn't asked Lyla for the key. He slapped his forehead with the heel of his hand. He would ask tomorrow when he went back in to redo everything he had done today.

EMILY PULLED *To Kill a Mockingbird* out of her backpack and tried to tune out the noise of the younger kids clambering onto the bus after school.

"He shoved me," Justin shouted and pointed at Christopher.

"Justin, sit down," the driver growled.

"Sit here," Emily whispered to Christopher, patting the seat beside her.

Christopher shook his head, and Emily watched him walk to the middle of the bus and settle into a seat by himself.

"Can I help you?" the bus driver called out.

For a second Emily thought maybe he was talking to Christopher, but he wasn't. He was looking down the steps —at Isabella. "I'm looking for my cousin, Justin Taylor," she said.

Emily and the bus driver moaned in unison. "He's back there." The driver jerked his thumb over his shoulder.

"I'm supposed to go home with him."

"Poor you," the driver said and then chuckled. "You must be the new rider I was told about this morning. Get on. I'm about ready to leave."

Isabella climbed the steps and then clapped her hands together when she saw Emily. "I didn't know you ride this bus."

Emily grimaced. "I do now, since Sam graduated." *And since Grandma won't let me take her car to school.*

Isabella slumped into the seat beside Emily.

"So Justin Taylor is your cousin." Emily was still surprised by how everyone was related in a small town.

"Yep." Isabella turned her head and frowned. "Looks like he's picking on your little brother."

Emily turned around just as the bus lurched forward, but before she could say anything Isabella belted out, "Justin, leave that little kid alone or I'll come back there."

Justin crossed his arms and smirked. He towered over all of the other kids by a head or more. The kid had to be close to six feet.

Isabella shook her fist at him and then settled back down next to Emily. "They're renting a new place out in the country. The owners sold out to a bigger farm, leaving the house vacant. His mom has been pretty sick the last few years. His mom and my mom are sisters."

Emily looked out the window as the bus turned onto the highway.

"Speaking of my mom," Isabella said, "she said she saw you yesterday."

Emily wanted to groan but didn't. "Yeah." She sighed. "Boy, it's hot in here." She squirmed and fanned herself with a folder. "How come you have to go out to Justin's?"

"My mom's working a double shift."

"Oh." Emily didn't want to ask about Isabella's father because she didn't want their conversation to focus on fathers at all.

Isabella slumped in the seat. "Were Mrs. Stevenson and your uncle upset about the house?" Isabella's voice was low.

"Pardon?"

"You didn't know?"

"Know what?"

"My parents made an offer on their house and then, you know, backed out."

"Oh." No one had told Emily. "How come?"

Isabella plucked at the piping on the seat in front of them. "Because—didn't Ashley tell you?"

The bus stopped, and three little kids slowly made their way up the aisle and off the bus. "Lily Cunningham said something, but I didn't catch the details."

Isabella rolled her eyes. "That Lily. She doesn't even know. Ashley's the only one I've talked to." Isabella rubbed her eye. "Isn't that like her? You tell her something, hoping she'll tell a few people, important people like you, but then Ashley is so proper—or something—that she won't gossip at all."

Emily sat completely still as the bus stopped again. Finally, as it started up, she said, "That's Ashley for you."

All day she'd expected Isabella to mention that her parents had seen Emily with Christopher and her father at Jenny's Creamery. She thought Isabella would ask her about it, loudly, in front of a large group of people—around their lockers or in the cafeteria or maybe during English in front of Aunt Dana. But she hadn't. The bus stopped a third time. Maybe they would come to Emily's stop before Isabella had a chance to ask about her dad.

She shifted in her seat a little. "So." Emily paused. "What's up with your father?"

"He caused an accident last week. He'd been drinking."

"I'm sorry," Emily said. So far Isabella's story wasn't any different from Lily's.

"And he's a truck driver so he lost his job." Isabella looked like she was going to cry.

"Oh." So that was why they couldn't buy the house.

"We've lived in that dinky apartment for two years now. I'm so sick of it. I could just kill him." Isabella wedged her black, clunky shoe against the back of the seat in front of them.

Isabella's mom didn't seem mad at her husband yesterday. "How's your mom doing?"

Isabella snorted. "My mom is, like, the nicest person you'd ever meet. She's upset, sure. But she didn't yell at him or anything. She just said she was really sad and yes, upset, but that things would work out. Somehow. Some way."

Emily didn't respond.

"He had a drinking problem a few years ago but then quit. Or so he said."

Emily definitely wanted to change the subject. "How is choir going?" Emily asked.

Isabella sat up straight. "Fine. I had no idea your dad is from around here."

Emily rolled her eyes. "He's not. He's just passing through." Emily tilted her head to peer through the windshield of the bus. They were almost to the Carter place, almost home.

"Mom said he seems like a nice man."

Emily wrinkled her nose, wanting to say, *He's not*, but wanting more not to say anything at all. They rode in silence a few moments.

"Hey, Em." Christopher's voice came from behind her. "Look who's waiting for us."

She half stood, looking over the heads of the kids across the aisle. There was Dad, waving like a fool. The bus jerked to a stop, and she fell back into her seat. "See you tomorrow," she said to Isabella, quickly stuffing her book into her bag and then stepping over the girl's big shoes.

The bus door swung open, and Emily hurried down the steps. There was Dad, waiting to meet her.

"Hey, I got the job," he called out. "Where's Christopher?"

Emily glanced over her shoulder at Christopher, who was struggling with his backpack. "Come on," she hissed at him.

Isabella was smiling at her. She'd heard. Every student on the bus had heard Dad.

PETE TURNED THE TRACTOR slowly, checking over his shoulder to make sure the seeder was making the turn. The stubble from the harvested wheat was well trampled, and he had sprayed for weeds the week before. Seeding the winter wheat would take a few days. It was usually a good cash crop, as long as the weather and the price of wheat cooperated.

The plants would germinate and establish themselves before the first frost, if all went as planned. Then the stubble would insulate the green shoots through the winter.

He straightened out the tractor and headed down the next row. He was pulling the old twelve-row seeder that they'd had forever. He'd noticed on his way out to the farm this morning that the corporate farm had a shiny twenty-four-row seeder—attached, of course, to the big, new tractor.

Pete shook his head as if he could rattle away the thought, which was exactly what he wanted to do. There were more important things to think about. *Dana. The baby. The new house. Selling the old house. Finding the loan papers.* He'd gone through the boxes that were stacked in Dana's office, through his old tax returns, through his GED records, through everything he could find, but there were no loan papers anywhere.

He looked toward the sky. And he had the soybean crop to worry about. Clouds were roiling low in the muggy sky toward the east. Pete turned his attention back to the field. In the distance a figure walked toward him. At first he thought maybe it was Sam, but soon he realized it was Christopher coming through the stubble, trying to jog across the bumpy surface.

Pete slowed the tractor to a stop and opened the door.

"Can I ride along with you?" Christopher yelled over the sound of the engine.

Pete nodded, and Christopher hurried around to the other side, opened the door quickly, and then slammed it shut against the dust, grasshoppers, and noise.

"What's up?" Pete asked, shifting back into gear and then accelerating.

"Dad's at the house."

"And you're out here?"

Christopher nodded. "He was talking to Grandma. I said I needed to check on something. I couldn't stand being in the house anymore."

"What were they talking about?" Pete slowed as he came to the end of the row.

"Dad got a job in Harding."

Pete nodded. He remembered Kevin talking about a job.

"And he was talking about getting an apartment—in Bedford or in Harding."

"Oh," Pete said, not sure what else to say.

Christopher leaned back against the seat. "I don't really want to talk about all that. I just wanted to ride with you for a couple of rows."

"Okay." Pete started to turn the tractor. "How about one row and then back you go. I don't want anyone to get worried."

Christopher nodded and slumped back against the seat.

Pete kept his eyes straight ahead but felt like he should say something. "How are you feeling about having your dad around?" That was what Dana would ask. He glanced at Christopher.

"Weird."

Pete waited a second and then said. "How's that?"

"Ice cream was fun, and I like showing him around the farm." Christopher picked at the cuticle on his thumb and then shrugged. "Anything more than that feels weird."

Weird. Pete was pretty sure that was as much as he was going to get from Christopher.

CHARLOTTE TOPPED OFF Kevin's coffee, wondering if she should ask him to stay for dinner. Emily had gone up to do her homework, Christopher had escaped outside, and Bob said he needed to go check to see if he'd emptied the pan after changing the oil in his truck. Charlotte was pretty sure he had done that, but wanted an excuse to go out to the shed.

So far Kevin hadn't said a word about his intentions, just that he got the job and would soon be looking for an apartment. He'd been chattering away about his travels as if he hadn't talked with anyone in months.

"I like Nebraska better than Texas," he said. "I didn't when I was a teenager." He smiled almost apologetically. "I couldn't wait to leave."

A wave of sadness for Denise passed through Charlotte as he spoke. Denise was always the elephant in the room when Kevin was around.

He took another sip of coffee and was silent for a moment.

"Can you stay for dinner?" Charlotte asked, brushing imaginary crumbs off the tabletop.

"Oh, no," he said. "I should get going. In fact, I said I'd fix dinner for my buddy tonight."

"What are you having?"

Kevin shrugged. "Probably tacos." He smiled shyly.

Charlotte called up the stairs to Emily and told her to come down to say good-bye. Then she walked Kevin toward the door. "Christopher should be around. I'll just poke my head out and look for him."

As she walked across the lawn, Sam drove up the driveway, his window rolled down. "There's a storm coming," he said. "It's been in my rearview mirror all the way home."

"Your dad's here," Charlotte said. "He's leaving though."

Sam's face stayed slack.

"I'm just looking for Christopher so he can say good-bye," Charlotte said.

Sam rolled forward, and Charlotte headed toward the barn; as she neared the door, she heard Christopher calling for her.

"Here I am." He was climbing over the fence from the pasture.

"Where have you been?"

"Out in the field with Uncle Pete. I took the shortcut back."

She motioned him back to the house as Emily and Kevin came out the back door. Sam joined them in the middle of the lawn. As Charlotte approached, Sam said, "Guess, what—this job will pay for my tuition. I get half tuition plus a stipend that will more than cover the rest."

"That's great," Charlotte said.

Sam crossed his arms and grinned.

"You'll have to see how it all goes," Kevin said. "Remember, college isn't for everyone."

"Well," Charlotte said, aware that all three of the kids were looking at her. "That's a thought."

"I'm doing fine without it." Kevin had his hands shoved in the pockets of his pants.

"But you wanted to go, right?" Emily asked. "When you first decided to go to San Diego?"

Kevin frowned. "That was a long time ago. It's hard to remember." He gave Emily a puzzled look.

"When will you be back?" Charlotte asked, not wanting Emily to mention her mother's diary or any more of what she knew of her father from back then.

"I'm not sure," Kevin answered.

All three children looked downward. Christopher picked up a stick, Sam toed the grass with his shoe, and Emily started examining her fingernails.

"Kids," Charlotte said, "tell your dad good-bye and then go in and finish up your homework." She was going to have to take control of the situation. It was obvious that Kevin was as oblivious as ever.

One by one, they said their good-byes; there were pats on the back but no hugs.

"Go on back in the house." She walked with Kevin toward his car, and once the back door slammed behind the kids she turned toward him. "You can't just show up and then be in the area and not let the kids know when you're coming back."

"What are you talking about?" He looked defensive for the first time since he'd been back.

"Please make a plan. Let us know when you plan to stop by again. Thursday? Saturday? Sunday? Pick a day and I'll tell the kids, but as it is, you're stringing them along."

His face reddened. "I'll come Saturday then."

"Good, we'll see you then." Charlotte told him good-bye and headed toward the house just as thunder crashed in the distance. She looked toward the east. Dark, low clouds were scudding across the sky toward her. She should have asked him what his long-term intentions were, but she couldn't bear to do it. She was still hoping he would disappear again and she wouldn't have to deal with him or a possible custody fight, but his getting a job in Harding made that less likely. An imaginary conversation with Kevin about custody began to form in her head again, but the falling rain brought her back to the present as she hurried into the house.

Chapter Fourteen

Charlotte stood at the kitchen window, her hand holding back the sheer yellow curtain, and watched Emily stroll across the lawn, slightly swinging the bucket full of eggs. She wore her hair in a twist atop her head and a string of magenta costume beads around her neck. Her top was a floral print, and she wore a new pair of dark skinny jeans that came closer to her waist than the previous years' styles.

The girl certainly had a fashion sense all her own. She reminded Charlotte of her own mother, who, every time she left the house, had worn shoes that complemented her outfit and carried a handbag that matched. For much of her life she'd also worn a hat, and always lipstick. She was a townie, and it showed. Of course, styles had changed through the years, but Emily had that same sense of fashion with a gift for accessorizing, matching, and complementing.

Charlotte glanced down at her worn pink sweater and T-shirt and sighed. She stepped back from the window, turning her attention to Bob's oatmeal, as Emily came through the back door.

Emily put the bucket on the counter, turned on the water, and then began washing the eggs one by one. She hated to have dirty eggs in the fridge.

"Grandma," Emily said, placing an egg on the dishtowel laid over the countertop's fading Formica. "Isabella said her parents were going to buy Pete and Dana's house."

"Oh?" Charlotte left the wooden spoon in the pot.

"What did Uncle Pete say about it?"

"Just that the buyers backed out because of something to do with the husband's job."

Emily nodded and then headed to the pantry for an egg carton. As she came back through the door she said, "He lost his job with his trucking company because he hurt someone in a traffic accident."

"Oh, dear," Charlotte said. Everyone had their own troubles; that was for sure.

"But I think the reason she told me is because she wanted me to talk about Dad. Her parents saw us on Sunday at Jenny's Creamery." Emily placed the last of the eggs in the carton. "It was like she was trying to get me to talk."

"Misery loves company," Charlotte said.

"What's that supposed to mean?" Emily opened the refrigerator door.

"Just that someone who's going through a hard time likes to know that other people have hard times too."

Emily kicked the door shut. "Am I going through a hard time?"

Charlotte winced, wondering if she'd said too much. "It might seem to Isabella that you are."

"Well, I don't want to talk with her about Dad. She's loud, and she gossips." Emily opened the breadbox and pulled out a loaf.

Charlotte called down the hall to Bob that his breakfast was ready. It was hard to know how to respond to Emily because Charlotte didn't know Isabella.

A minute later Bob lumbered into the kitchen just as Christopher came sliding in from the family room in his socks.

"Whoa," Bob said, putting his hands on the shoulders of his grandson.

Christopher grinned and then pulled away. "Hey," he said, "has anyone seen my math homework?"

Charlotte shook her head, and Bob ignored him. "Check the pantry," Emily said.

"Be serious," Christopher snapped.

"I am." Emily spread peanut butter on her whole wheat toast. "Go look." She glared at her brother.

He slid to the pantry doorway and then came back out, his eyes down, holding a stack of papers in one hand and a box of cornflakes in the other. "I must have put it down when I was getting my bedtime snack last night."

Bob chuckled as he sat down at the table. "You're getting as forgetful as I am, young man."

Charlotte handed Bob his bowl of oatmeal. Adolescence and old age had a few things in common. She put the pitcher of milk on the table, and Christopher and Emily both joined their grandfather.

"Where's Sam?" Bob asked.

"He doesn't have class until eleven this morning."

"Doesn't mean he shouldn't be up and moving."

Charlotte agreed.

"Hey." Christopher sloshed milk onto the table as he filled his spoon. "Is Isabella a bully like Justin?"

"No," Charlotte said as Emily answered, "Yes."

"It must run in the family," Christopher said, and then shoved the spoon in his mouth.

Emily put the remaining half slice of her toast back on her plate. "She's not a physical bully like Justin; she's more like a verbal bully. She talks about people, and I can be pretty sure that she talks about me behind my back too."

CHARLOTTE SLIPPED on her shoes as Emily grabbed her book bag.

"Where are you going?" Emily slipped her bag over her shoulder.

"The mailbox."

"Now?"

Charlotte nodded.

Emily pushed open the door and let it slam shut behind her—right in front of Charlotte and Christopher.

"What's with you?" Christopher asked, preceding Charlotte out the door.

"It's bad enough that I have to ride the bus to school, but Grandma, you've been walking with us to the bus stop all the time lately." She quickened her step.

Charlotte tried to remember how often she had walked the kids to the school bus. She hadn't done it yesterday morning. Or last Friday. Emily was definitely letting either her dad or Isabella, or both, get to her.

Toby came running from the direction of the pasture, nipping at Christopher's heels. Christopher grabbed a stick and twirled it through the air toward the windbreak. Toby shot ahead.

"Yuck!" Emily yelled.

Alarmed, Charlotte started to jog. "What is it?"

"Something dead."

Christopher ran ahead. "It's just a raccoon."

"Don't let Toby get close to it." Charlotte was out of breath by the time she reached the children. Toby stood barking, held back by Christopher.

She took the dog's collar and said, "Sometimes raccoons have rabies."

"No foam on its mouth," Christopher said, leaning down over the carcass. "Or other indicators."

"Still," Charlotte said, "we don't want to take any chances." She moved ahead with Toby. "I'll come back and get the raccoon after you get on the bus."

"Remember what Silas Maynard said?" Christopher stepped away from the dead animal. "That he'd found lots of dead animals on his place?"

"We haven't had many," Charlotte said, "at least not any more than usual." She walked with a stoop so she could hold Toby's collar; she wished she had brought the dog's leash. They'd had that dead crow and then a dead squirrel in the yard, and she had smelled skunk the other night, but that didn't mean it was dead.

Charlotte put an envelope into the mailbox and raised the red flag as the bus came over the knoll. She told Emily good-bye and then gave Christopher a quick hug. "I'm praying for you," she said as the bus came to a stop.

"Pray hard," Christopher whispered and then followed Emily up the stairs.

Charlotte scanned the windows of the bus. In the middle, each at a window separated by several seats, sat Justin and Isabella. Neither one of them acknowledged her.

Five minutes later she chained Toby and started to the house to ask Sam to get the wheelbarrow to move the raccoon, but as she reached the shed she heard Bob's and Pete's voices and veered off to the side.

"I'm going to give Bill a call and see what he can do for us," Bob said.

"Dad, wait, would ya? We have a little more time."

"Are you sure you've looked everywhere for that paperwork?"

"I'll look again," Pete said.

Bob had already faxed the paperwork from the twenty-year loan they had paid off several years ago. Now he just needed the current paperwork.

"Find it," Bob said. "Or I'm going to go over and tear your house apart."

AFTER LUNCH, Charlotte called Grandma Maxie and asked if she would like to come out to the farm and can tomatoes the next day. The older woman accepted the invitation but said she wouldn't be able to make it until after lunch because she had a morning doctor's appointment.

Charlotte went through her canning supplies in the pantry. She'd put up peaches and green beans two weeks before and, as she suspected, needed more lids and rings.

Later, as she entered the city limits, she decided to stop

by Fabrics and Fun and see Rosemary. It had been a couple of weeks since she'd seen her sister-in-law. She wasn't sure if Pete had told his aunt about the baby yet, so she was determined not to say anything if Rosemary didn't bring it up.

Charlotte stopped her Ford Focus in front of the shop. Cutout scarecrows and pumpkins decorated the windows of Fabrics and Fun. As Charlotte pushed through the front door, a spicy potpourri greeted her.

"Well, well." Rosemary looked over the rims of her reading glasses, a smile creeping across her face. "How are you?" She hurried around the counter and embraced Charlotte.

"Good." Charlotte returned the hug and then stepped back, taking in the bright fall colors of the fabric that filled the shop.

They chatted about the children for a minute and then Rosemary said, "I heard Kevin's in town. I can't remember who told me." There was a sparkle in her eye; obviously she did know but didn't want to say. "Someone saw him at Mel's Place."

Charlotte nodded. The whole town probably knew by now.

"What does he want?" Rosemary sounded the way Charlotte felt.

"To see the kids."

"Nothing more?" Rosemary tugged on the tape measure around her neck.

"I'm not sure." Charlotte groaned. "But he just got a job in Harding."

"Oh, dear," Rosemary said. "Is there anything I can do?"

"Pray," Charlotte said softly. "For wisdom mostly. And for Emily; so far it seems to be the hardest on her."

"You got it." Rosemary put her arm around Charlotte again. "What's up with Em?"

"There's the stuff with Kevin. And then she's having a hard time with a girl at school."

Rosemary raised her eyebrows.

"Isabella."

"Dobbs?"

Charlotte nodded.

"Now *there's* a family that's having a rough time right now." Rosemary seemed to always know what was going on with people in the community. "Her mother shops in here pretty frequently. She was in yesterday and told me their sad story."

Charlotte nodded again. "Emily told me part of it."

"I hope she's being nice to Isabella because the girl could use a good friend right now."

"Actually Emily's afraid to get very close to the girl, afraid she's going to gossip."

"Maybe you can encourage Emily," Rosemary said, tugging on the tape measure around her neck. "And don't expect the worst from Isabella."

Charlotte tilted her head.

Rosemary chuckled. "You do that sometimes."

"I do?" Charlotte was trying not to sound offended.

"Yeah. Remember Sig Campbell's granddaughter?"

"Rayann?"

"That's the one. You had the hardest time befriending her."

"Rosemary, do you remember that Rayann had an older brother that Emily was absolutely smitten with and that there were lots of things going on behind my back?"

Rosemary's face reddened. "I'd forgotten that. Well, you know what I mean. Be nice to Isabella if you can."

They chatted for a few more minutes. Charlotte was sure Pete and Dana hadn't told Rosemary about the baby because she hadn't brought it up. Rosemary was quite the talker; so until they wanted the whole town to know, it was probably better not to tell her.

Charlotte said good-bye to her sister-in-law and headed to the grocery store for her canning supplies. But she felt unsettled. Did she come across as an old ogre to more people than just Rosemary? Maybe she'd set a bad example for Emily in interacting with other people. Charlotte sighed.

THE NEXT AFTERNOON, Grandma Maxie arrived promptly at one o'clock wearing a short-sleeved shirt, a billowy skirt, and sandals and no hose. It was already ninety-five in the shade. Even though Maxie was dressed for the hot work, Charlotte hoped she wouldn't end up with heatstroke.

Charlotte led her into the kitchen. Boxes of tomatoes she had picked the last couple of mornings covered the table. She had water boiling to skin the tomatoes, and she had already sterilized the jars, rings, and lids.

They visited while they worked, starting with their favorite shared topic: Dana and Pete's baby.

"I imagine Dana will go to Harding to deliver," Grandma Maxie said as she waited for Charlotte to plunge the tomatoes into the boiling bath.

"I would think so too." A few women still had their babies at Bedford Medical Center but not many, and Dana had already gone to a doctor in Harding for her first prenatal appointment.

"And Pete will be at the birth?"

"I hope so," Charlotte said, lifting the wire basket of tomatoes from the water and shaking the handles, draining the water as the steam heated her arms, neck, and face.

"Things certainly have changed," Grandma Maxie said.

Charlotte smiled. "Dads have been involved in births now for years. I know women who were having first babies around the time Pete was born who had their husbands in the delivery room with them."

Grandma Maxie smiled. "Not Bonnie. I think Chuck would have liked to have been in the delivery room, but Bonnie had to have a C-section and her doctor wouldn't let him in the operating room."

"Oh really?" Charlotte swung the basket to the table and emptied the wrinkled tomatoes onto a big platter.

"She had lots of problems carrying Dana and then more problems later. She lost three babies after Dana was born—all pretty early." Grandma Maxie paused as she picked up a paring knife and a tomato. "Actually, she might have lost more than that; those were just the ones she told me about."

Charlotte put a new batch of tomatoes in the basket and lowered it into the boiling water. She had no idea Bonnie had lost so many babies. Then she sat down at the table and began peeling tomatoes alongside Grandma Maxie. "Is Bonnie worried for Dana?"

"She doesn't seem to be. She's just excited about the baby. Dana's healthy—a lot healthier than Bonnie was back then."

Charlotte worked in silence for a moment, not wanting to pry.

"She had some kidney problems. Kidney stones and other things."

"Oh." Charlotte sighed. "That's a relief." She had been afraid maybe there was a hereditary problem that would affect Dana.

Grandma Maxie smiled, and there was an awkward silence.

"How was your doctor's appointment?" Charlotte asked.

"Just fine. My blood pressure has been high, but Dr. Carr started me on a new medication. I want to be healthy for this baby."

Charlotte smiled, smashing the peeled tomato down into a jar.

"Healthy enough to babysit. That's my goal."

Charlotte nodded and then thought of how wiggly and squirmy baby Will was now, but Grandma Maxie was still strong. Charlotte pushed another peeled tomato into the jar. Grandma Maxie was a great role model; Charlotte hoped she would be able to help with her great-grandchild.

Three hours later, they finished the tomatoes. "This kitchen has to be at least a hundred twenty degrees," Emily moaned as she passed through on her way outside with an apple in her hand.

"Now, don't exaggerate," Grandma Maxie said. "It can't be hotter than a hundred fifteen." The woman hadn't wavered throughout the work.

Charlotte checked the lids, pressing down on the metal. Each was perfectly sealed. She ran down the basement steps and came back up with a cardboard box; then she filled it with a dozen jars. "Here you go," she said, putting the box on the table.

"Oh, there's no need." Grandma Maxie stood and headed to the sink. "I just wanted to help."

"No, I insist," Charlotte said.

"Honestly, I won't use all of those." Grandma Maxie washed her hands at the sink.

"You can make soup," Charlotte said.

"How about if I take them by Dana's?"

"Sure," Charlotte said. "And I'll give them more too."

"This might help make cooking easier for her in the next few weeks," Grandma Maxie said. "Or maybe I'll use some of the tomatoes to make spaghetti sauce for them."

"I'll carry them out to your car," Charlotte said, lifting the box.

Grandma Maxie opened the back door and popped the trunk of her Taurus sedan. Charlotte carried the box of jars, and they made their way down the walkway. But as Charlotte lowered the box into the trunk, Grandma Maxie said, "Oh, dear," and pressed her hands against the side of her car.

"What's the matter?" Charlotte asked.

"I'm feeling a little lightheaded, that's all."

"I'll go get a glass of water," Charlotte said.

"No. I'm fine. Really." She opened the door to her car and sat behind the steering wheel. "I'm fine now." She smiled up at Charlotte. "I'll see you soon."

Chapter Fifteen

Friday afternoon Sam pushed away from the Mac, glancing up at the right-hand corner of the screen. It was 5:15. He had spent four hours updating the website. The English department secretary had unlocked the door for him again. Maybe Russell had been right about the hours this job took. He had already put in fifteen this week. He'd be making only five dollars an hour if he wasn't careful.

He stood and slung his backpack over his shoulder.

"All done?" Lyla asked, standing in the doorway of her office.

"Yep."

"Got Friday night plans?" she asked.

He smirked. He supposed he could be one of those lame alumni and go into Bedford to watch the football game. "Not really," he answered. He missed having friends around. Jake was off at the University of Nebraska, and Paul was in the Army. For a split second he thought of Arielle, living in the dorm at Grace U in Omaha, making lots of new friends and probably going on lots of dates.

"Some friends and I are going out for pizza. Want to join us?"

Sam tilted his head, trying to imagine Lyla's friends.

"They're all friends from church."

"Church?" Sam said.

She smiled. "You know—a place where people worship together."

Sam chuckled. "I know what church is." He looked around the room. Had Grandma been praying or something? Maybe there was an angel hanging around that had tapped Lyla on the shoulder. "That would be cool," he said. "Going out for pizza."

"We're meeting at Pino's," Lyla said. "It's just off the highway about ten blocks from here."

Sam nodded.

"Do you want to follow me?" she asked.

"No, I can meet you there."

"Cool," she said, heading to the hallway. "I just have to stop by the English office for a sec. Wait for me in the parking lot at Pino's."

SAM WAITED AND WAITED in the parking lot, watching groups of people in twos and threes and fours enter the pizza place. A Honda Civic turned into the parking lot. He squinted in the dim light. It was Lyla. She pulled into the spot next to him and waved, and then both of them climbed from their cars at the same time.

"Come on," Lyla said. "Everyone else is inside." She handed him a key as they walked. "I finally got this from the secretary."

"Thanks." He shoved it into his pocket and then opened the door for Lyla; she hurried through, scanning the room, and then she waved. "They're in the corner." Sam followed her through the crowded room.

Lyla said hello to the group of eight. "This is Sam," she said. "He's taking Russell's place at the newspa—oh, you're here, Russell." She smiled. "I didn't know you were coming tonight." He was in the corner with his hood up.

"Hi, Sam," people called out as he sat in the closest chair he could find. Then they went around the table, introducing themselves. There was one obvious couple, Sarah and Jack, and a young woman named Penny who had a pretty smile. He couldn't remember anyone else's name—except Russell's.

The conversation soon turned to the school newspaper. "It's a bear," Lyla said. "Being an editor is harder than I thought it would be." She blew upward, and the wispy hair around her face floated up. Everyone laughed.

"Cute, huh?" Russell said quietly, leaning toward Sam. "Just don't get too attached."

He wanted to say he wasn't attached to her at all, that he knew nothing about her, but he didn't.

"What church do all of you go to?" Sam asked Russell.

Russell put his hands up, palms out. "I don't. I just come for pizza on Fridays."

"Grand Island Community Church," Sarah said from across the table.

Sam nodded. It was a big facility on the edge of town.

"Jack and I are the college group leaders." Sarah's voice was kind. "And anyone is welcome to join us for pizza on Friday nights or come to services on Sunday. Right, Russell?" She gave him a teasing look.

"Yep." He pulled his sweatshirt hood farther over his

forehead. "You always make me feel welcome." The guy was smiling, just a little.

Sarah asked Sam if he had a home church, and he told her about Bedford Community Church.

"We know your youth pastor," she said. "Jason Vink." She went on to explain that she and Jack had been on a retreat with Jason the year before. "He's a great guy," she said, and Sam nodded.

When the pizza arrived, Jack said a prayer, and everyone bowed their heads. Sam stole a look at Lyla. With her eyes closed, she looked angelic.

Sam ate slowly, content to listen to the others chatting, but soon he was telling Sarah and John about moving to Nebraska from San Diego. Lyla must have been listening because she said, "I'm from the West Coast too—Seattle. Not quite as sunny as California." She smiled at him for half a second, and then it was obvious she was looking past him at Russell. Her smile dissolved.

Russell pointed out that pretty much everyone at the table was from somewhere else, adding that he had come from Delaware. Everyone was silent for a minute, and then Sarah said that she and Jack had met in Oregon, at seminary. "So we're sort of from the West Coast too," she said, "although we're both from the Midwest originally."

At seven o'clock Sam's cell phone vibrated, and he dug it out of his pocket. It was a text from Emily. *Are you going to the game?*

I don't think so, he texted back; then he said to the group, "I need to get going. What's my part for the pizza?"

"Our treat," Jack said.

"No, really." Sam pulled out his wallet.

"Chill," Russell said. "They pay every Friday. It's like alms or something to them. You know, 'alms for the poor.'" He laughed. "Meaning, the poor college students."

"Thank you," Sam said. He told everyone good-bye, saving Lyla for last, saying he would see her on Monday.

She nodded. "Thanks for coming," she said and then looked past him again. He left feeling unsettled. The get-together was fun, but Lyla was one mysterious girl.

PETE SAT DOWN on the couch next to Dana, who was stretched out halfway.

He put his hand on her leg. "Sweetie," he said, shaking her gently, "I need to talk with you about something."

"What?" She sat up straighter.

He'd waited long enough, too long probably to tell her about the loan mix-up. Why was it so hard to be honest? He knew why. He didn't want her to know what a loser he was.

"What is it, Pete?" She reached for his hand.

"You know that loan I told you about a few months ago?"

"For the new house?"

He shook his head. "No. For the farm."

She nodded.

"Well, I seem to have lost the paperwork." He rushed on. "I looked through Mom's files and through my boxes here. I can't find it anywhere."

"Did you call the bank?"

"That's just it. They say it's a twenty-year loan and a big balloon payment is coming due, but Dad swears they're looking at old records, at a loan he paid off years ago."

Dana let go of his hand. "That doesn't make any sense."

"The main bank in Grand Island has all the loans now; it's not handled by the Bedford branch. That's why I need our paperwork."

"Did you look in the right-hand drawer of my desk?"

"Noooooo." He drew the word out. Why would he have looked there?

"Remember? I told you I unpacked that shoe box of documents, and then you told me to leave the rest for you to do."

Pete jumped to his feet and took off down the hall, wishing he'd told Dana about this nightmare a week ago. He yanked the drawer open. Dana had put dividers and folders in the drawer, and he began thumbing through them. In the third folder was the paperwork he needed. He pulled it out and sank down on the chair, leafing through the pages. There it was: six months, no balloon payment. He lifted the paper to his face and kissed it.

"Yes!" he shouted as he headed back to the living room. "Dana, thank you, thank you, thank you!"

She was sprawled out on the couch again, one eye open.

He bent down and kissed her forehead. "You have saved my you-know-what," he said, kissing her a second time. She smiled faintly.

Pete grinned, feeling better than he had in weeks. He'd call Dad and tell him he'd found the paperwork, and Dad would fax it to the bank tomorrow, even though it would be Saturday.

"Want to go to the game?" He knelt down beside the couch.

Dana whispered, "Not really."

"Do you want to eat?"

"Later," she mumbled.

Pete headed to the kitchen to call Dad, but no one answered the house phone. He was probably outside checking up on the work Pete had done earlier. He'd rather talk to Dad than leave a message. He might as well take a shower and then think about what to cook. He should probably go to the store, but maybe he could throw something together from the pantry. He could make pancakes for dinner if he needed to, although Dana would probably want a better meal than that.

He grabbed a towel from the hall closet as the front doorbell rang. He hesitated. It was probably some solicitor. The bell rang again. Maybe it was someone interested in the house. He shuffled back to the living room and opened the door.

Grandma Maxie grinned at him over a cardboard box.

He quickly took it from her and staggered for half a second under its weight. "What's in here?" he asked. "Bricks of gold?"

Grandma Maxie smiled. "Better. Canned tomatoes and a batch of spaghetti sauce."

"Sweet," Pete said, heading toward the kitchen. "Come on in. Dana's snoozing on the couch, but you can wake her up."

"Let her sleep." Grandma Maxie followed Pete into the kitchen.

"Excuse the mess," he said. "I was just going to clean up." Breakfast dishes filled the sink, and a box of Wheaties was still on the counter.

"Let me help," Grandma Maxie said. She had hot water running in the sink before he could protest.

He set the cereal box back in the cupboard and then pulled a clean dishcloth from the drawer. "Excuse me," he said to his grandmother-in-law, and then he stepped in closer to the sink and held the cloth under the water for a second. Dana was always reminding him to wipe down the table and the counters.

"Doesn't look like you've had any dinner," Grandma Maxie said.

Pete shook his head. "Dana was asleep when I got home."

"Do you have noodles?"

Pete turned from the table and began opening drawers, not quite sure where Dana kept that stuff. "We have this," he said, holding up a box of large pasta shells.

"That will work. How about cottage cheese? And mozzarella cheese? Or even cheddar cheese?"

Pete opened the fridge and started rummaging around, which wasn't hard since there was hardly anything in it. He found half a tub of cottage cheese and checked the date. It was good by two weeks. Then he opened the meat drawer and pulled out a quarter brick of Colby cheese, holding it up. "We have this."

Next, he rummaged in the vegetable drawer. "And lettuce and..." He held up what he'd found. "Five tomatoes and three cucumbers from the farm."

Grandma Maxie grinned, her hands submerged in the soapy water. "Dinner, it is. Now you go get cleaned up, and I'll get everything started in here. We'll let Dana sleep."

A few minutes later, Pete leaned against the shower wall, letting the water cascade over his face. He hadn't realized how tired he was until Grandma Maxie started dinner. It was such a relief to have her help.

He turned off the water, toweled down, and hurried into the bedroom. As he dressed he heard distant thunder. "Not again." He waited. It wasn't getting any closer. He hoped the storm was heading toward Harding and not toward the farm. He sat down on the bed, picked up the phone, and dialed the familiar number again.

Dad answered with a gruff, "Hello."

"It's me. Hey, it's not raining out there, is it?"

"Nah," Dad said. "It's not raining. It's pouring. Cats and dogs. I just got soaked on my way in from the shed."

"Are you kidding?"

"Why would I be kidding?"

Pete groaned. "Hey, I have some good news." He stood, hoping his voice would sound stronger. "I found the paperwork for the loan."

Dad grunted and then said, "It's about time. Bring it out tomorrow so Mom can fax it."

"That's what I was planning—"

Dad hung up before Pete finished. He held the phone to his ear for a moment, stunned, and then put it in its cradle and padded down the hall.

Dana was stirring in the living room, and Pete knelt beside her. "Your grandma is here, cooking us dinner."

Dana grimaced. "I'm not feeling too hot. It's like I'm having cramps or something."

"For how long?"

"The last half hour or so. Off and on. I thought they'd go away."

"I'll call the doctor," Pete said, heading for the kitchen.

There was no need for alarm, no need to upset Grandma Maxie or cause Dana to be any more stressed than she already was. That definitely wouldn't be good for the baby.

He stepped into the kitchen, "Grandma," he said, expecting her to be at the sink or the stove. She wasn't. She was on the floor, on her back with her foot tucked under her leg in a funny position. Shocked, he dropped down beside her, relieved to find her pulse and see that her chest was rising and falling with each breath.

She opened her eyes. "Oh, Pete," she said, turning her head one way and then the other. "I think I fainted." She started to move and then winced.

"Does anything hurt?" he asked.

"My leg."

He felt it through her pants leg. "Stay put," he said. "I'm going to call 9-1-1." *And then Mom.* He exhaled as he grabbed the phone. He needed help.

EMILY SAT IN THE STANDS next to Ashley trying to hear what Isabella was saying. She caught the words "Justin" and "staying with my aunt is a big bummer." The cheerleaders made a pyramid down below, and one of them, in the middle row, faltered. All of them came tumbling down. Isabella began to laugh loudly, covering her mouth with her hand, and then she snorted.

Ashley clapped for the cheerleaders. "Good job!" she called out just as Troy rounded the corner of the bleachers. He scanned the student section, and Emily stood and waved.

As he started up the stands thunder crashed in the distance.

"Oh, no!" Isabella stood, turning toward the sound. "They're going to have to call the game."

"It's miles away," Ashley said. "It was really faint."

"No, it was practically right overhead!" Isabella's voice was really loud.

"Sit down," someone barked behind the girls.

Troy smiled as he approached Emily. "Hi," she said, trying to ignore the chaos around her. "I thought you had to work."

Emily took a step away from Isabella and sat down. Troy plopped down beside her. "They called and told me to come in a couple of hours later; they scheduled too many dishwashers."

"So you have the really late shift?"

He nodded. "I'll need to leave in a little while but thought I'd stop to see you first."

Emily's heart skipped a beat as another bolt of lightning flashed across the sky.

Isabella screamed.

"She is so getting on my nerves," Emily whispered to Troy. He put his arm around her for a quick second and then let it fall between them. She thought he might reach for her hand, but he didn't.

"I'm going to the bathroom—where's it's safe." Isabella stepped down a row. "Come on!"

Emily rolled her eyes.

"I was going to get some popcorn anyway," Ashley said quietly to Emily. "Want some?"

"No thanks," Emily said.

Isabella skipped down the steps. "You'd better run for cover," she called out to the band members who were waiting to walk down to the field for the halftime show. "Don't go out there. You'll get struck by lightning."

The band members ignored her and started filing down the bleachers one by one in their wool uniforms. Emily couldn't imagine how hot they were. The two boys with the tubas around their necks looked like they were about ready to pass out.

"Do you work tomorrow?" she asked Troy.

"Yep. And Sunday."

"When do you do homework?"

He grinned. "During my breaks—sometimes."

The first members of the band reached the field and began to play the music from the classic movie *Chariots of Fire*.

"Cool," Troy said. "I love that movie. It's one of my favorites."

"Me too!" Emily would never have guessed he liked it. She was about to ask him when he'd first seen it when it registered that Isabella was at the bottom of the bleachers screaming her name.

"Emily!" She was waving her arms back and forth. "Emily! Your dad's here!"

Emily stood slowly as her face grew warmer and warmer. As if in a dream she stepped past Troy to the steps and started descending them. She couldn't hear the band. She was vaguely aware of Troy following her. She could barely see her father at the corner of the stands, watching her.

She reached the concrete walkway at the bottom of the

bleachers. Now Isabella was grinning and pointing at Dad, and he was smiling too.

Emily walked past Isabella and stepped past Dad, around the corner of the bleachers, hoping the whole school hadn't witnessed the horrifying scene. How could Isabella have done that to her? "Hi," she said to her father.

"I thought I would come to the game, for old times' sake."

Emily gave him a puzzled look.

"I used to come to the Bedford games because..." He paused. "Your mom was a cheerleader."

Emily nodded. Now her father had a puzzled look on his face. She'd read about him coming to the games in her mother's diary—but she wasn't going to tell her father that.

Troy stopped at her side and nudged her. She gave him a half smile and then said, "Dad, this is my friend Troy."

Troy shook Dad's hand and said he was pleased to meet him, and then Isabella stepped forward and bellowed, "And I'm Emily's friend Izzy. I was on the bus the other day and saw you then." She swept her arm wide. "And this is Ashley."

Dad said it was nice to meet both of them, and everyone stood around for a moment. Emily tried to discreetly text Sam, writing, *Dad's at the game! Where are you?* Then Troy cleared his throat and said he needed to get going, that he had to work until 2:00 AM in Harding.

Dad looked around. "Is Sam here?"

Emily glanced down at her phone and decided that Sam must be driving and actually obeying Grandma's mandate. "No. And I don't think he's coming."

"What about Christopher?"

Emily shook her head. Christopher had stayed home because he was afraid Justin would pick on him; now Emily saw Justin down on the grass beyond the end zone playing football with other middle school students, knocking all of them silly.

"Well, I'll just watch the game," Dad said.

"You can sit with us," Isabella said, still hovering.

"You know," Emily rubbed her fingers across her forehead. "I'm not feeling so hot. Do you mind giving me a ride home?"

"Ummm, sure. But you should call your grandma and let her know."

Emily nodded.

"Hold on," Isabella said. "I was going to see if I could get a ride. And Justin."

Emily wrinkled her nose.

"I'm staying at my aunt's house again."

"Oh," Emily said. "Well, we're going now."

Isabella's body sagged. "I'll go get Justin." She stomped away.

None of this was going the way Emily planned.

"Emily, is everything all right?" Dad stood at her elbow.

"Yeah, my head hurts; that's all. And I feel a little queasy." A second later Emily's phone rang from a number she didn't recognize. She almost didn't answer but on the last ring decided to take it.

It was Grandma. "Em, can you get a ride home?"

Emily turned away from her father. "What's the matter?"

"I'm here helping Pete. Dana is having some pain, but I think everything is okay. However, Grandma Maxie broke her leg."

"Oh, no!" Emily said.

"If you can get a ride that would help."

"Grandma." Emily took a couple of steps away from her father, aware that Ashley had struck up a conversation with him. "Dad's here. I'm not feeling well, and he said he could take me home."

There was a pause, and then Grandma said, "Okay."

"But then Isabella said she and Justin need a ride."

"That's fine too."

"Can I come to the medical center instead?" Emily's voice squeaked.

"Emily, let your dad take you home, and then make sure Christopher gets to bed at a decent time."

"Grandma—"

"What?" Grandma sounded really tired and not concerned at all, for a change, about Emily spending time with Dad.

"Nothing. I'll see you when you get home."

"Bye, sweetie." Grandma's voice sounded a little nicer. Emily said good-bye and pushed END on her phone as Isabella approached, dragging Justin by the collar.

"Come on," she screamed at him, "or I'm going to make you regret this."

"You're hurting me," Justin whined.

Isabella let go, and he collapsed on the ground. When he got up, Isabella nodded at Dad. "This is Christopher's father. He's going to give us a ride home."

Justin pushed up the sleeves of his sweatshirt and kicked at the grass.

"Come on," Emily said. "Let's go."

Chapter Sixteen

Charlotte stood as Bonnie and Chuck Simons approached the sliding glass doors of Bedford Medical Center. Bonnie led the way, practically flying through the automatic doors. "Where is she?" she called out to Charlotte.

"Dana?" Charlotte asked.

Bonnie nodded.

"Dr. Carr is examining her right now."

"Pete should have taken her to Harding, to the ER."

Charlotte sat back down and patted the chair next to her.

"I should go back," Bonnie said.

"No, you shouldn't." Chuck pointed to the chair. "She's with the doctor. And Pete is with her." Chuck looked at Charlotte for verification, and she nodded.

"How is Mom?" he asked.

"Okay. You can see her, I'm sure. Dr. Carr is going to wait until tomorrow to set her leg."

Chuck headed to the receptionist's desk.

"What did Dana say?" Bonnie asked. "Is she in a lot of pain? Pete hardly gave me any information at all."

"Between Dana and Grandma Maxie, he was pretty busy," Charlotte said.

"I can't bear for Dana to go through what I did, especially with her first baby. At least I had her before I lost the other ones," Bonnie said.

Charlotte nodded in sympathy.

Chuck returned. "Mom's just down the hall."

Bonnie stared at him.

"Are you coming?" Chuck asked.

Bonnie turned to Charlotte with a searching look.

"I'll come get you if Pete comes out," Charlotte said. "Go on. Tell Grandma Maxie I'm praying for her."

"And for Dana?" Bonnie asked, standing.

"Of course," Charlotte said.

CHARLOTTE CLOSED HER EYES as she prayed. She was tired, and it was stuffy in the clinic.

"Mom." It was Pete.

Charlotte's lids flew open, and she stood. "How is she?"

"Dr. Carr says things are okay. She needs to keep her feet up for a few days. He said sometimes when the baby is implanting into the uterine wall there's some bleeding and cramping."

Charlotte nodded. She'd heard that before.

He sank into the chair beside her, and Charlotte sat back down. "Bonnie and Chuck are here. They're in with Grandma Maxie."

"Do you think Bonnie will want to stay with Dana?"

"I'm sure of it," Charlotte said, smiling.

"I need to work tomorrow. Do you think she'll think I'm awful if I do?"

"No. Talk to Dana about it first; she'll understand." Actually Bonnie would probably be happy to have Pete out of the way, but she didn't want to tell him that.

CHARLOTTE OPENED the car door as she turned off the key and then yawned. The kitchen light shone through the window. She hoped no one had waited up for her. It was well past midnight. She pulled her sweater tight against the chill with one hand as she hurried through the darkness. The sky was clear now, and stars studded the sky.

She yawned again as she opened the back door and stepped inside, hung her sweater, turned off the kitchen light, and started down the hall.

"Grandma?" It was Christopher's voice. He was standing in the doorway to the family room. "Is Aunt Dana all right?"

"You should be in bed."

"I couldn't sleep." He stepped closer. "Is the baby okay?"

Charlotte reached out and drew him to her. "So far they're both fine. Dana needs to rest and put her feet up."

"I was researching my medieval project some more. It made me worry."

Charlotte wasn't sure that was the best topic for Christopher right now. "We have to trust God," Charlotte said. "This is why each baby is so precious and valuable. This doesn't just happen by chance. It's a miracle."

"What if the baby doesn't make it?"

"Pete and Dana will be really sad—all of us will. But then

there will most likely be another baby." Charlotte knew she had no way of knowing, but it was likely. Dana hadn't had trouble getting pregnant the first time.

Christopher pulled away from her.

"Let's pray for Aunt Dana and the baby, and for Uncle Pete. And for Grandma Maxie. She's in a lot of pain right now," she said.

Christopher nodded, and Charlotte bowed her head, "Dear Lord," she prayed. "Please take care of Dana and the baby. Please help us to trust you..."

LIGHT STREAMED THROUGH the lace curtains of the bedroom as Charlotte opened one eye, trying to focus on the digital numbers of the clock. Her other eye flew open. *7:38.* She hadn't slept this late in—she couldn't remember the last time.

She flung the cotton blanket to the middle of the bed and swung her feet onto the floor, grabbing her robe from the end of the bed and starting down the hall, trying to remember what was on her to-do list for the day.

Bob sat at the kitchen table, the *Bedford Leader* spread out in front of him.

"Good morning," Charlotte said, grabbing a cup from the shelf.

"Well hello, sleepyhead." Bob peered at her over the top of his glasses.

Charlotte poured her coffee and took a sip. Nine times out of ten she was up before Bob. "I didn't get to bed until after midnight."

"Excuses, excuses." Sam's voice came from behind her.

Charlotte spun around and laughed. "You're up early for a Saturday."

"I have a lot to do today." He grabbed a mug too.

"Is Christopher up?" Charlotte sat down at the table across from Bob.

"I haven't seen him," Sam said.

"What about Emily?"

Sam shrugged.

"Have you heard from Pete?" Charlotte asked Bob, wrapping her hands around her mug.

"He's out in the Sawchuck's Quarter—has been since I got up."

Charlotte shook her head. "What did he say about Dana?"

"I haven't talked with him," Bob said, folding the paper. "I just saw him out there."

Charlotte stood. "I'm going to get dressed and go see how everything is."

"You could just call Dana," Sam said as he walked toward the family room. "That would be easier."

"Not if she's sleeping," Charlotte answered, already heading down the hall.

AS CHARLOTTE grabbed her sweater, Bob said he thought he'd go with her. She knew it would take him a minute to get his boots on, so she went into the family room to continue talking with Sam. He was on the computer, as she expected.

"What time did you get home last night?" she asked.

"Right after you left." He clicked the mouse, and the page changed.

"Were you working that late?"

"Nah." He turned toward her. "I went out for pizza with a bunch of college students from a church in Grand Island."

"Really?" Charlotte was surprised. She didn't know he was getting to know any of the other students at the college, let alone people in a church group.

"Now I'm friends with all of them on Facebook." He smiled.

Charlotte stepped forward. He was on the page of a young woman with carrot red hair. "Who is that?" she asked.

"Lyla. She's my boss."

"Oh."

"Don't get all weird, Grandma. It's not even like we're friends—except on Facebook. I just went out to pizza with her and her peeps."

Peeps. She knew from Emily that meant people. Friends.

"Char! Let's go." Bob's voice boomed from the mud porch.

"We'll be back in a few minutes. Tell Em and Christopher where we went." She started to leave. "And tell Emily that Dana was okay last night. She's probably worried." Although it seemed as if she had been more worried about Kevin giving Isabella a ride home than she was about Dana, the baby, and Grandma Maxie.

Charlotte and Bob walked along the highway for a quarter of a mile and then cut across the wheat stubble that

Pete hadn't planted yet, toward the lower field. Pete's pickup was parked in the far corner, off the dirt road, but Charlotte couldn't see Pete.

"Do you know if he brought the loan paperwork with him?" she asked.

"I told you I haven't talked to him. But he probably didn't or he would have dropped it off at the house." Bob stretched out his stride, and Charlotte struggled to keep up. She hadn't realized he could still walk so fast.

"There he is," Bob said, pointing to the far end of the field. "Down by the creek." He was stooped over.

Bob led the way between two rows of soybean plants. The soil was damp, and there were drops of rain on the leaves of the plants. The sky was completely blue now without a cloud in sight. And the morning air was crisp, as if autumn might arrive after all.

They were within fifty yards of Pete when Bob stopped in his tracks and Charlotte nearly bumped into him. "What in the world is he doing?" Bob asked.

Charlotte stepped beside him. It looked like Pete was picking leaves off the plants, one by one. Bob started walking again, chuckling to himself. "Pete!" he called out. "You're going to have to work twenty-four hours a day to make a difference. Plus you'll have to haul those leaves off or the fungus will still spread."

Pete straightened his back. "Plucking the leaves off is the only good advice I've gotten so far."

Bob nodded. "But how are you going to make a dent in all these acres of soybeans?"

Pete yanked his leather glove off his right hand and

pulled his hat from his head, raking his fingers through his thin hair. "So what do you advise? 'Cause I don't have any other ideas." Pete looked as if he might cry.

"How's Dana?" Charlotte asked, stepping forward, putting her arm around her son's shoulders.

"She didn't have any more spotting or cramping during the night."

"That's good."

"Bonnie is going to stay with her all day. Chuck stayed at the clinic last night with Grandma Maxie."

Charlotte nodded. That had been decided before she left last night.

Pete leaned down and wrapped both of his hands around spotted leaves and pulled them from their stems, tossing them into a pile behind him. "If we lose this crop we're toast," he said.

"Pete." Charlotte hated it when he talked that way.

"We'll lose the farm." Pete straightened up, stretching his back.

Bob cleared his throat but didn't say anything.

"You're tired," Charlotte said to Pete. "Come back to the house and have some breakfast and a cup of coffee. Then we'll send the kids out to help," she added. "There are some old burlap bags in the barn. They'll be perfect to put the leaves in."

Pete bent down to pull some more leaves, acting as if he hadn't heard a word she said.

"Pete." Charlotte knew her voice sounded annoyed.

"I'll be there in a few." Pete didn't look up. "And that would be great if the kids could help."

Bob cleared his throat. "Did you bring the paperwork for the loan?"

Pete's face fell as he looked up. "I forgot it." He tossed down a clump of leaves. "I'll go get it later; I promise."

"I can go in," Charlotte said.

Bob shot her a disapproving look.

"It's on the dining room table," Pete said. "At least I think that's where I left it last night."

Bob rolled his eyes, and as they walked away he muttered, "He's not ready to take over the farm."

"He found the paperwork," Charlotte said. Pete had told her last night that he'd had no idea Dana had filed some of his papers. Still, he hadn't handled the document properly in the first place; that was for sure. She understood Bob's position on that. But Pete, like everyone, needed to be allowed to learn from his mistakes.

CHARLOTTE PUT A CUP of coffee in front of Pete as he sat down at the table with Emily and Christopher at breakfast.

"How's Dana?" he asked.

"She was asleep, but Bonnie said she was doing fine." Charlotte didn't want to tell him how worried Bonnie seemed. Charlotte didn't see how that could be good for Dana at all.

"And you found the paperwork?"

"It was on the table." She'd faxed it as soon as she got home. One of them, probably Bob, would call first thing Monday morning to follow up.

Pete poked at his eggs. "I've lost my appetite," he said, taking his half-full plate to the sink.

"Come on, kids," Bob said to Emily and Christopher, who were finishing up their pancakes. "We're going to get those burlap bags from the barn and head out to the crops with Pete."

The kids quickly rinsed their dishes, not talking as they worked.

"Come on, guys," Pete said, clapping his hands together. "Let's go save the farm."

Charlotte followed them out the door just as Kevin pulled into the driveway.

Emily didn't even try to hide her groan. "I forgot he said he was coming by today."

Christopher slowly walked over to meet him as Kevin parked his car.

"We're going to go work in the field with Pete," he said, opening the car door. "Want to come?"

"Am I invited?"

"Sure." Pete scowled. "The more the merrier."

"We're going to save the farm." Christopher pointed to Bob, who was coming out of the barn with a pile of burlap bags.

"That bad, huh?" Kevin smiled at Pete.

"Getting that way." Pete turned toward Emily. "Do you know anyone looking to make some extra money?" he asked.

Emily shook her head.

"How about your friend?" Kevin asked. "The one we took home last night. She said she needed to find some work."

Emily wrinkled her nose and shook her head.

"I bet her brother—"

"Cousin," Emily corrected.

"—would be a good worker. He's a big kid."

"Are you talking about Justin Taylor?" Christopher's voice had a hint of horror in it.

"Yeah. Justin—right, Em?" Kevin had a confused look on his face.

Emily was rolling her eyes.

"The ones who live down the road?" Pete took the bags from Bob. "That'd be really convenient. They could get off the bus with you guys."

Emily and Christopher both looked at Charlotte with big eyes.

"We'll talk about it later," Charlotte said to the kids. "Now work hard for Uncle Pete. This is important."

Chapter Seventeen

Sunday after church, Charlotte stood in the greeting area. Pastor Nathan had asked for prayer for Grandma Maxie, so Hannah and Melody were both asking her for details.

"And I heard Dana isn't feeling well either." Melody's voice was low.

"She's been a little under the weather," Charlotte said, not wanting to say anything that would give away that her daughter-in-law was expecting, wondering if Emily had said something to Ashley. Hannah must have remembered that it was still mum's-the-word about Dana because she didn't add anything to the conversation, but she put her hands together, indicating that she was praying for Dana and the baby.

Just as Charlotte started to nod a thank you, Melody elbowed her and whispered, "Look who's here. Behind you."

Charlotte turned. Kevin was standing outside the church, leaning against the white clapboard siding, just to the side of Pastor Nathan.

Her heart began to race, and she glanced around. Emily stood off to the side with Ashley, Hunter, and, surprisingly, Isabella. Emily's eyes were wide and round as she stepped in front of the group and quickly turned to face her friends. Obviously she had spotted her father too. Charlotte said, "Excuse me" to Hannah and Melody and wiggled her way around the other people toward Kevin.

His face brightened when he saw her, and he stood up straight, pushing the sleeves of his wrinkled white dress shirt up to his elbows.

"Nice to see you here," she said. "Were you here for the service?"

He nodded as she realized it was a stupid thing to ask.

"I sat in the back," he said. "I saw you and the kids in front, but I was late."

"Charlotte." Pastor Nathan's hand was coming toward her, and she shook it.

"I'd like you to meet..." She hesitated. "The children's father. This is Kevin."

Pastor Nathan shook Kevin's hand vigorously and then patted his back. "I can't tell you how much I enjoy your kids."

Charlotte winced at the words *your kids*.

"Thank you," Kevin said.

Charlotte inhaled. Did he think he could take any credit for Sam's, Emily's, and Christopher's behavior? They were doing well in spite of Kevin—not because of him.

"What brings you to town?" Pastor Nathan asked.

"I took a job in Harding." Kevin glanced at Charlotte. "So I could be closer to the kids."

A questioning expression passed over Pastor Nathan's face, but he didn't pursue the subject. "Good, good," he said. "It's so nice to have you here today."

Charlotte scanned the crowd. Emily and her friends were nowhere in sight. Perhaps they had gone to the fellowship hall for cookies and punch.

She heard Sam's voice behind her and turned. He was speaking to Jason Vink. "I met a couple who know you," he said. "In Grand Island. They help out at the community church there." Charlotte stepped back, hoping to hear more of the conversation and get more details of the outing, but Kevin was pointing to Christopher, who was waving from the sidewalk.

Charlotte followed Kevin down the steps.

"Are you coming out for lunch?" Christopher asked his dad. "And then taking us out for ice cream?"

"You're welcome to come for dinner," Charlotte said. "Bill and his family are joining us."

"I told my buddy I'd help him work on his car," Kevin said. "But thank you."

"What about ice cream?" Christopher said.

"It's not in my budget right now." Kevin looked at the ground. "I'll take you out once I get paid."

Christopher scowled, and Kevin looked uncomfortable for a moment. Then he said, "How about if I come out tomorrow after school? I could help pick the soybean leaves again."

"Sure," Christopher said, but he didn't sound very convincing.

"In fact," Kevin said, "did you ask your buddy down the road if he wants to help?"

"He's not my buddy." Christopher crossed his arms.

"There's his cousin."

Sure enough, Emily and her entourage were walking toward them.

Kevin's voice was loud. "Hey, Em, did you tell your friend that Pete is looking for some extra hands?"

"Um," Emily's eyes were big again. "I didn't."

"Oh, hi, Mr. Slater," Isabella said. "What's up?"

The kids milled around Charlotte, Christopher, and Kevin. In a minute Kevin had invited all of them to help out the next day. Ashley said she was working at her mom's café and wouldn't be able to.

"You're Melody's daughter?" Kevin asked, stepping back. Ashley nodded.

Emily stiffened. It was obvious to Charlotte that Emily felt out of sorts. Kevin had no idea how his daughter was feeling, but as much as Charlotte wanted to protect Emily, she couldn't control this situation. Neither could Emily.

Sam ran down the stairs, and then Bob appeared with a cookie in his hand. Charlotte shook her head. "Ready to go home? Bill and Anna will get there before we do if we don't hurry," Charlotte said.

"Let's go," Emily said, pulling away from her friends, saying she would see them tomorrow.

"What about tonight?" Isabella asked. "I'm going to youth group with Ashley. She said everyone sings first—which sounds really cool. Are you coming?"

Emily shrugged. "Maybe."

Christopher hugged Kevin good-bye, and Sam walked with his dad toward his old beater.

Charlotte wished she could read Kevin's thoughts, could know why he had come to church and what he was scheming. Who could know what Kevin Slater was up to?

CHARLOTTE SCOOPED Will into her arms, rubbing her face over his soft, fine hair. He giggled and threw his head back. "How many teeth do you have now?" she asked him. He smiled.

"I see four," she said, "two on the top and two on the bottom."

"And a lot of drool." Christopher stood beside her on the lawn.

Will squirmed in her arms and reached for Christopher, who took him, hoisting him onto his hip. At nine months, Will was busy, crawling everywhere and pulling himself up to stand.

"He'll be walking soon," Charlotte said to Anna, who was holding the diaper bag and a cake pan.

"I know, I know," she said. She had on a floral dress and heels, and her dark hair fell around her shoulders.

"May we take Will to the barn?" Madison asked as Christopher handed Will to her.

"I don't think that's the best idea," Anna answered, taking the baby.

Emily gathered the girls and offered cheerfully, "Let's go see if we can find some kittens."

"Have you told the girls about Dana's pregnancy?" Charlotte asked, taking the cake pan from Anna.

"We thought we'd wait." Anna shot a look at Bill.

"Until she's further along," he said, stepping away from the car.

"Bill talked to Pete last night," Anna said. "I bet they're wishing they hadn't told so many people about the pregnancy already, huh?"

Charlotte decided not to respond to Anna; Bill piped up

to fill in the gap. "Boy, they've really had a rough spell, haven't they?" he said. He slipped out of his sports jacket as they entered the house. "Smells good," he added, inhaling the aroma of the roast finishing in the oven. Then his voice grew louder. "It sounds like you've had some drama too. Pete said Kevin's around."

"Sam's in the family room," Charlotte whispered.

Bill raised his bushy eyebrows. "So?" His voice was normal.

"Your dad's in there too." Charlotte put the cake on the counter. "Why don't you go tell him hello?"

She was sure Bill didn't get her hint, but he sauntered into the other room anyway.

"What's Kevin up to?" Anna's voice was low. "Does he want the kids back?"

Charlotte didn't want to talk about it with Anna or anyone else, except maybe Hannah or Bob. "I don't know," she said.

"Have you hired a lawyer?"

Charlotte shook her head.

"Well, maybe it would be for the best." Anna pulled the carafe out of the coffeemaker. "How old is this?"

"I'll make a new pot." Charlotte took a filter and the can of coffee out of the cupboard, trying to ignore Anna's comment. Reacting to it wouldn't do any good.

"I hardly got any sleep last night. Will's teething again." She yawned. "Anyway, it would be good for Kevin to step up and take responsibility. You and Bob aren't getting any younger."

As Charlotte cringed, she was thankful she had her back

to her daughter-in-law. "Tell me," she said, controlling the tone of her voice, "how are the girls doing in school?"

Anna took the bait and began chatting about Jennifer and Madison, about how well Jennifer was reading and about how Madison was learning her multiplication tables. Ten minutes later when the children returned from the barn she was still talking about their accomplishments as Charlotte asked Christopher and Emily to finish setting the table.

"DO YOU WANT to take the car in to youth group?" Charlotte asked Emily at six forty-five.

Emily sat on the family room couch, her feet tucked beneath her, reading *To Kill a Mockingbird*.

"Emily?" Charlotte sat down beside her.

"Huh?" Emily's head jerked.

"I asked if you wanted to take the car to youth group. I don't need it this evening."

"Oh, I can't go," she said. "I need to finish this. We're supposed to discuss the ending tomorrow."

It looked like Emily had about a third of the book left to read. "Where are you in the story?" Charlotte asked.

"Have you read it?" Emily asked.

Charlotte nodded.

Emily tilted her head. "Really?"

"Several times. It's one of my favorites."

"Why?"

"Well, I didn't grow up in the thirties in a small town, but I did grow up in a small town. And I was a young adult when Harper Lee wrote the book. I read it, and then your grandfather and I saw the movie at my dad's theater in Bedford. It really opened my eyes."

Emily was quiet.

"What do you think of the story?" Charlotte plumped one of the couch cushions.

"I like Scout; she's a lot of fun. And Atticus is pretty cool. It's like he does the right thing without making a big deal about it. It's part of who he is."

Charlotte nodded. "And he values people—all people."

"Someone was talking about that in class the other day."

Charlotte continued, "It's hard to see people for who they are, not for who we think they represent. But it's important that we do."

Emily nodded and started reading again, but as Charlotte stood, she said, "I wish I knew more about Dad."

Charlotte sat back down.

"Most of what I know about him is from Mom's diary, from when he was eighteen and nineteen."

Charlotte nodded. "You could ask your father about himself."

Emily scowled. "That would be awkward."

"It might not be in a few more months." Charlotte stood again. She rubbed the back of her neck as she headed into the kitchen. She wished Emily would go to youth group. She thought about how she used to force Denise to go, but she and Bob had chosen their battles with Sam and Emily. Sunday morning services were mandatory, but youth group was optional.

Charlotte began unloading the dishwasher. She was pleased that Dana taught *To Kill a Mockingbird* in junior English and that Emily was enjoying it. Emily was right; Atticus did value people. It would be interesting to know what connections Emily made between the book and her own life.

Chapter Eighteen

Monday after class Sam sat in front of the row of computers in the newspaper lab.

"I thought you said you posted the new text on the website." Lyla stood in the middle of the newspaper lab, her hands on her hips.

"I did," he said, rolling forward in his computer chair.

"It's not there."

"What?" It was there when he checked on Friday.

"Take a look." She spun around and marched into her office.

Sam quickly logged onto the website, clicking to the articles. Sure enough, all the ones he had posted Friday had disappeared sometime over the weekend. He reposted the articles and went back to working on the layout that one of the staff people was supposed to be doing but wasn't because she hadn't shown up and Lyla had begged him to do it, saying she didn't have time. He rechecked the website, and the text had disappeared again. He slapped his hands down flat on the table. The quickest way through this was to go down to the computer lab and ask Russell for help. He grabbed his backpack and was at the door, thinking Lyla hadn't seen him, when she called out, "Where are you going?"

"To get something to eat," he answered. He would do that too.

"Would you bring me back a latte? Nonfat."

"Sure," he muttered, quickly slipping through the door.

When he got to the computer lab, Russell wasn't in sight. He asked the woman at the first desk if she'd seen him, and she said he would be back in about an hour. He was off selling ads for the newspaper, she said, adding, "I think he went to the mall."

Sam stood at the doorway of the lab for a moment. He could go back upstairs and waste more time or go eat somewhere for an hour or go track down Russell, get his answer, eat the sandwich he'd packed in his backpack before he left the farm, get Lyla a latte, and then get back to the lab. He ran down the hall and out to the parking lot.

HE FOUND RUSSELL in the middle of the mall, chatting away with a guy behind a printing supply kiosk.

"It would be a great place to advertise," Russell said. "Just think of all the printer ink that students use."

"I actually don't have that many students as customers," the man said.

"Exactly." Russell smiled. "You need to be advertising with us."

Sam thought of the two hundred and fifty pages of printing each student was allotted at the college. Russell didn't seem to be mentioning that.

"Most of the students at the college commute," Sam said, sidling up to the kiosk.

Both the man and Russell looked at him, surprised.

"And their families buy ink—probably lots of it. Their younger siblings—or maybe their kids if they're older—do a ton of printing. So you wouldn't just be advertising to the students but to their families. Just think of how many households that would include."

"Good point," the man said. "But who are you?"

Sam blushed. "I work for the newspaper. I'm the tech guy. I was just hunting Russell down to ask him a question."

"Give me a few minutes to think about it," the man said. He looked at Russell. "Come back after you've talked to some of the other businesses, and I'll let you know."

Russell stepped away from the kiosk and turned to Sam. "What's up?"

Sam explained his problem, and Russell snorted. "You probably just previewed the document. You have to save it." He slapped Sam's back. "You don't know that much about the website, do you?"

Sam blushed.

"But you were pretty good on that sale."

"What sale? The guy hasn't bought anything yet," Sam said as he looked up and down the mall. There was a lotion kiosk and a perfume kiosk and one with curling irons and hair straighteners. The other direction, there was one selling stationery, including greeting cards and calendars, and then the ink-jet kiosk. "Have you thought about grouping the ads?" Sam asked.

"What?"

"Splitting the ads," Sam answered. "For example, dividing

one ad between the beauty-products kiosks and another one between the shops that are business-related. These are smaller enterprises. A full ad is expensive, right? But a half or a third might be affordable."

Russell slapped Sam on the back. "Slater, you're brilliant!" He started toward the kiosk selling lotions. "Hey, you can ask me about the tech stuff anytime."

LATE THAT AFTERNOON Emily wiped the sweat from her brow and then straightened out the burlap bag that was tied to her belt. The fabric had an old oily smell to it that made her head ache, and it was already half full of the spotted soybean leaves and getting really heavy.

"Can't we empty these bags?" Justin whined.

"Pete went to get his pickup," her dad answered. Emily could tell he was getting annoyed with Justin.

"Suck it up, Justin," Isabella called out from a row away.

Justin stood tall and snapped, "Make me."

"Justin, that's enough." Dad's voice was low but firm, and his response surprised Emily.

Instead of looking relieved, Isabella had an annoyed look on her face, and Justin looked hurt.

They worked in silence for a few minutes. Emily's eyes started to feel a little buggy as she searched the plants for the spotted leaves. The sun was bright, and she saw spots on all the leaves. She had to concentrate to identify the fungus.

"Hey!" Christopher's voice came from the next row over. Emily stood. Justin had jumped on his back.

Dad's face reddened and Isabella flung her bag on the

ground just as a horn honked in the distance. It was Pete in his pickup at the edge of the field. "Bring your bags over and dump them," he yelled, cupping his hands around his mouth. "Then it's time for a break. Grandma sent lemonade and cookies."

Justin slid off Christopher's back and started running, jumping over plants, his gangly arms flying in all directions.

"Hey!" Pete boomed. "Knock that off!"

Justin stopped.

Pete sounded like an automated recording as he said, "Step over the plants carefully."

By the time the rest of them reached the truck, Pete had Justin off to the side of the field and was speaking to him. As much as she wanted to eavesdrop, she couldn't make out any of the conversation. She opened the passenger side of Pete's truck and took out the basket of cookies, the two thermoses of lemonade, and the stack of paper cups.

"What a nice grandma you have," Isabella said, grabbing a cookie.

"I agree," Dad said, taking one of the thermoses and unscrewing the lid.

"Christopher." Emily held the basket out to him, but he had his eyes glued to Justin and Pete. "Christopher," she said again.

He turned back to the basket, took a cookie, and then muttered, "Now *after* school is as bad as during school."

"He'll stop. Pete won't let him keep working if he keeps acting like that," Emily answered.

Christopher shook his head. "Uncle Pete's worried about his crop and his house and his baby—not about me."

Emily started to say that wasn't true, but then Pete was

beside them. "Just five minutes," he said. "Then we have to get back at it."

After the break Uncle Pete and Dad worked side by side, then Emily, Isabella, and Justin. Christopher was on the other side of Pete, as far away from Justin as possible as they worked the outer six rows of the field.

"Do you start your new job tomorrow?" Pete's voice boomed across the field.

Dad's voice was quiet and subdued. "I was supposed to, but the foreman called and said it won't be until next Tuesday now."

"That's too bad," Uncle Pete answered. Then he turned toward Emily. "How was school today? Minus your favorite teacher."

"Fine."

"What's wrong with Mrs. Stevenson? Does she have the flu?" Isabella stood up straight, stretching her back.

Pete stood too, taking his hat off. "No—"

"Well, kind of," Emily interrupted, catching Uncle Pete's eye. He had his hat in his hand and was wiping his forehead with the back of his gloved hand.

"Right." He smiled a little. "It's some sort of virus."

"That's funny." Isabella bent down again and plucked a leaf. "Because some of the girls at school are betting that she's pregnant."

"Who?" Emily said.

"Wouldn't that be *whom*?" Isabella had a smart-aleck look on her face, although she was incorrect.

"Whatever." Emily stuffed a handful of spotted leaves into her burlap bag.

"Oh, Lily Cunningham. Some of those girls."

Pete had his head down. Emily expected that Isabella's next words were going to be a direct question asking if Aunt Dana was in fact pregnant.

"Did you finish the book?" Emily asked, lowering herself to her knees. Maybe scooting along would be better on her back than bending over.

Isabella shook her head. "I'm going to tonight."

"The first draft of our essay is due tomorrow."

Isabella's face contorted. "I thought it was due on Wednesday."

Emily shook her head.

"Hey, Pete," Isabella called out in her booming voice that could probably be heard in the next county. "Can you talk to that wife of yours? Tell her my essay is going to be late 'cause I'm working for you."

"No. Can. Do," Pete said. "We're almost done for the day. You'll have plenty of time to write it."

A classic pout appeared on Isabella's face, her full lower lip jutting out and her big brown eyes wide. A streak of dirt creased her forehead under her spiky bangs.

"What book did you just finish?" Dad asked Emily.

"*To Kill a Mockingbird.*"

"Your mom really liked that book."

Emily pretended that she hadn't heard. Why would Dad mention Mom now?

"My back is breaking," Justin wailed from the next row over.

"Half an hour more," Uncle Pete called out. "Then we'll call it a day—and you can let me know if you're game for tomorrow."

"It's kind of funny to hear the youngsters complain about their backs," Dad said.

Pete laughed. "I know what you mean. They have no idea." Her uncle sounded amiable toward Dad for a change. "We're going to have to pick up the pace if this is going to make a difference." Dad stood straight and surveyed the field.

"Probably," Pete said.

"I can come out in the morning and work all day." Dad's voice was low, and Emily could barely make out his words. Uncle Pete was nodding his head and smiling in Dad's direction.

Emily turned her attention back to the plants.

"Hey," Isabella said, "did I tell you my dad got a job in Harding?"

Emily shook her head.

"He's staying with my grandparents and working in some kind of factory place."

"Really." Emily wondered for a moment if it was the same place Dad was going to work, but that would be too much of a coincidence.

"He can't drive, but he can ride his bike there." Isabella snorted. "Isn't that humiliating?"

Emily didn't answer. The weirdest thing about Isabella was how willing she was to talk. If Dad had caused an accident, lost his job, and now had to ride a bike to get around, Emily wouldn't be broadcasting it. She hadn't even told anyone except Ashley the story of Dad leaving their family when she and her brothers were little. And she really hadn't told Ashley what was going on now.

Emily sighed, plucking another leaf and stuffing it into the burlap bag and then stealing a look at her father. He was on his hands and knees now too, and the soybean plant he was next to was up to his chin. Emily had thought Isabella was gossipy, but maybe it was just that she liked to talk—about herself as much as others.

"WHY IS THIS PRINTER so slow?" Lyla asked, clicking the toe of her black pointy boot against the linoleum. She stood with one hand hovering over the printer at the end of the table of computers, her other hand grasping her cup of latte.

"Give it a minute," Sam said.

"I don't think it's working."

"I'm sure it is." He stood.

"I need to proof these articles. Now." Her eyes were drilling him. "I like hard copies." Her hand was opening and closing quickly.

The printer made a noise and then stopped.

"See? I told you it wasn't working." She exhaled dramatically.

Sam stepped around her to the printer. The yellow light was blinking. "It needs paper," he said.

"Oh." She spun around to the cupboard and pulled out a ream as Sam grabbed his backpack and headed to the door. "Isn't this your job?" she called out. "To keep the paper loaded?"

"'Fraid not," he called out, hurrying out into the hall, bumping into Russell.

"Hey, what's the hurry?" Russell grabbed him by the arm.

"I wouldn't go in there if I were you." Sam jerked his head toward the door.

"Lyla?"

Sam nodded.

Russell laughed. "I can handle her."

Sam pulled away, and Russell asked if he was going to be around the next day. "Yep."

"Can I stop in and run some ad ideas by you? You were brilliant."

"Sure," Sam said. Maybe Lyla would target Russell instead of him.

AS CHRISTOPHER WALKED beside his father back to the farmhouse from the field, he grabbed a piece of tall grass growing in the ditch along the dirt road and folded it into a whistle. The noise was sharp and clear.

"That's so lame, Slater," Justin said. Christopher could hear him coming, his feet shuffling in the dirt.

Christopher sidestepped, moving closer to his dad.

"Chicken," Justin hissed.

Christopher ignored him, and Justin ran ahead.

"He sure seems to have a lot of energy now for being so tired in the field," Dad said.

Christopher blew into his grass whistle again, watching as, up ahead, Justin covered his ears.

"Is your aunt going to come get you?" Emily asked Isabella.

"I have no idea," Isabella said, skipping a few steps in front.

"Maybe Uncle Pete can give you a ride home." Emily glanced back at Christopher. *And soon,* she mouthed. Pete had driven his pickup ahead to dump the spotted leaves on the burn pile.

Christopher half expected Dad to offer Justin and Isabella a ride, but his dad kept his mouth shut, much to Christopher's relief.

"Want a look at the barn, Dad? I didn't show it to you the other day," Christopher said as they cut through the pasture. Justin was already at the wire fence, climbing over it.

"Sure." Dad followed Christopher across the field. Christopher dodged cow pies as they walked to the back of the barn. Christopher opened the door, Dad stepped in, and both stood squinting for a second until their eyes adjusted.

"That's quite a stack of hay," Dad said.

Christopher nodded. "It's for the horses and the calves. The round bales outside are for the cattle." He walked to the middle of the barn and pointed to the calf pen. "That's where we keep the sick calves and the bummer lambs. I had a lamb for 4-H this year. His name was Magic."

"That's cool," Dad said.

"And Sam had a calf that he really liked. We all took turns feeding it, but it died anyway."

"That's too bad." Dad sounded like he really meant it. "I never lived in the country when I was a kid."

Christopher looked at his father for a minute, at his

short hair and the wrinkles around his eyes. He couldn't imagine his father as a kid, but still he said, "I think you would have liked growing up on a farm. I do. I'd hate to live in town."

Dad's eyes flickered a little, and then he looked up at the rafters of the barn. "There's a nest up there."

"Lots of them," Christopher said. "They're barn swallows."

"Sounds like a mess." Dad was looking all around the barn now.

"They're pests, according to Grandpa. But I like how they swoop down, and how much they like the barn." Christopher scratched his arm.

"Speaking of pests." Dad was walking toward the big barn door as he spoke. "What's up with Justin?"

Christopher sighed. "He's been picking on me forever."

"What happens when you stand up to him?" Dad pushed the latch on the door.

Christopher didn't answer.

"*Do* you stand up to him?"

"Not really," Christopher muttered, following Dad out the door.

Justin was throwing a stick to Toby over by the house. Dad closed the door and sat down on the bench just outside the barn, patting the wooden seat beside him. "When I was coming out here I was feeling uneasy." Dad paused. "A little afraid, to be honest."

"Why?"

"Oh, I don't know. Afraid I'd do or say the wrong thing." Dad smiled a little crooked smile. "I have a track record of that, you know."

Christopher nodded in agreement.

"Anyway, I finally decided I needed to just do it, be brave. Do the right thing."

Christopher didn't respond.

"Would you stick up for someone else? Say, if Justin was picking on someone at school?"

"Sure," Christopher answered. "One time he was picking on Dylan, and I told him to knock it off."

"How'd that go?"

Christopher shrugged. "Okay. He stopped bugging Dylan and started bugging me again." He stood, not sure how Dad could help him.

In the distance, Justin lobbed the stick across the driveway toward the barn, and Toby came rushing after it. Didn't Toby know not to play with Justin Taylor? Christopher jumped up from the bench and grabbed the stick as Toby came racing toward it. He hid it behind his back as Toby barked and ran in a circle.

"Christopher, don't tease her," Dad said.

"I'm not," he answered. "I'm protecting her from Justin."

Toby barked again.

"That's not funny, Slater," Justin shouted. "Give the dumb dog the stick."

"Throw it," Dad said quietly.

Christopher did, lobbing it over the fence and into the pasture, as far away from Justin as possible.

Chapter Nineteen

The last light of the day was fading as Charlotte pulled onto the street toward Pete and Dana's house. She hoped a quick visit would cheer everyone up.

Charlotte balanced the two pie carriers in her hands as she walked up the steps to their door, put one down, and knocked softly.

"Coming!" A moment later Bonnie flung the door open, and Charlotte stepped inside. Dana was reclining on the couch and gave her a wave, saying, "Hello."

"Pete's in the shower," Bonnie said, and then she added, "Oh, two of your pies, I assume. How thoughtful."

Charlotte followed Bonnie into the kitchen. "How is Grandma Maxie doing?"

"Good. And Dana's going back to school tomorrow—"

"She is?" Charlotte placed the pie carriers on the kitchen counter.

"The doctor says she should be fine." Bonnie lowered her voice. "But I'm not so sure." Bonnie lifted the lid on one of the carriers to peek inside. "I'm going over to Grandma Maxie's in a few minutes, and Chuck will go home so he can get back to work."

"How much longer will you be in town?"

"Probably just a few days. Maxie is getting around with crutches. I'll come back over every few days and do her grocery shopping and that sort of thing."

"I can help too," Charlotte said.

"Oh, you have enough to do." Bonnie lifted the apple pie out of the carrier.

"Not too much that I can't help Maxie," Charlotte said. She treasured the woman and would like to do what she could to help.

"I'll take Chuck and Grandma Maxie the peach pie," Bonnie said. "They'll be thrilled."

Pleased, Charlotte slipped back through the kitchen door.

"Can you visit for a few minutes?" Dana asked.

Charlotte said she could and sat down on the love seat. "Your mom said you're going back to school tomorrow."

Dana nodded. "Dr. Carr said there wasn't any reason not to. I could be up now, but Mom won't let me."

"Won't let you what?" Pete stood in the doorway, his hair wet.

"Get up." Dana laughed. "She has dinner in the oven for you, and your mom brought dessert."

Dana sat up, and Pete sank down onto the couch beside her as she reached for his hand. He didn't seem to have heard a thing about dinner or the pies.

"How are the soybeans looking?" Charlotte asked.

"I don't think picking the leaves is going to make a difference." Pete let go of Dana's hand. "Kevin said he'd come out again tomorrow, but I don't think he should."

"Why not?" Charlotte felt her neck tighten.

"Every time it rains the fungus spreads. Frank says the same thing is happening to his crop."

"What does Silas say?"

Pete shook his head. "That the fungus spreads every time the corporate farm truck goes by." He grimaced.

"Maybe he's right."

"Pete."

"I'm serious, Mom. Something's causing this."

"Animals could be spreading it—and the excessive rain we've having. Surely there's a natural explanation for this." Charlotte folded her hands around her knee. "It doesn't hurt to have Kevin come out." She could tolerate Kevin if it meant helping save the crop.

"I don't want to pay him if it's not going to do any good," Pete said.

"Oh." Charlotte conceded that he had a good point.

"And there's no reason to pay Justin to pick on Christopher either."

"Was it bad in the field today?" Charlotte's neck tightened more.

Pete nodded. "I think Kevin wanted to belt the kid."

In the distance, thunder crashed.

Pete moaned. "You can bet it's raining—pouring—out at the farm."

Charlotte sat back against the love seat. "Everything is going to work out."

Pete's eyes were heavy. "Everyone keeps saying that." He glanced at Dana, and she nodded. "Speaking of which, the bank officer didn't return my call today. I even gave him my cell number—but nothing." He sighed. "I'll call again tomorrow."

Charlotte tried to look encouraging, but unless the bank acknowledged the mistake, the payment was due in two more days. If Pete didn't get to the bottom of the mess immediately, Bob was going to drive to Grand Island again and make a scene. Pete pulled his hand away, stood, and started toward the kitchen, but then he stopped.

"Mom, could you call Kevin? Tell him not to come out."

Charlotte stood too. "Okay."

"See you tomorrow," he said, disappearing into the kitchen.

"He's been like this the last few days." Dana stretched her legs out again. "It's not like him."

Charlotte agreed. Pete was feeling all the responsibilities of being an adult for the first time in his life. His happy-go-lucky days were over; now he would have to figure out a way to cope—like every other responsible person did.

WHEN CHARLOTTE returned home, Christopher was sitting at the kitchen table with his social studies book in front of him, chewing on the eraser of his pencil, and staring at the wall.

"Hey," Charlotte said, stepping toward the table.

He startled and dropped the pencil. It bounced on the table and then fell to the floor.

"Hey, what?" he said, bending over.

"How's the homework coming?"

He straightened and yawned without covering his mouth.

"Need some help?"

He shook his head. "I'm too tired. I'll get up early in the morning and do it."

"How about a glass of milk and a cookie before bed?"

"Sure," he said, closing his book with a thud.

Charlotte poured the milk, put two snickerdoodles on a plate, and sat down beside him.

"How is your project coming along?"

He took a bite of cookie. "Fine."

"When is it due?"

"Friday." Christopher wrapped his hand around his glass of milk. "But I'm almost done."

"How was it, working on the crop with Justin?"

"Same story," Christopher said. "He hassled me as usual."

"Well, I think Uncle Pete isn't going to have him come work anymore."

"Why not?"

"He doesn't think it's going to make a difference."

Christopher swallowed. "What's Uncle Pete going to do about the crop? He has to pay for his house."

"Something will work out." Charlotte waited a second while Christopher took a swig of milk and then said, "Maybe you should try to be more assertive with Justin."

"Dad told me the same thing, kind of."

"Oh?" Charlotte said.

"At least I think that's what he was getting at."

"There are verses in Ephesians that speak to us about protecting ourselves," she said.

Christopher shoved the last of the second cookie into his mouth. "Really?" He spat crumbs as he spoke.

"The verses talk about putting on the full armor of God—truth, peace, faith, and the Word. All those things help us protect ourselves."

"How?" Christopher stood and headed to the sink with his glass and plate.

"What do you need from God to help you stand up to Justin?"

Christopher shrugged.

"Let's take truth," Charlotte said. "The truth is that God made you to be you, and he values you very much. He doesn't want someone to abuse you."

Christopher tilted his head and closed one eye but didn't answer. A moment later he hugged her and said he was going up to bed to read. She sighed after he left, reached for the phone, and dialed Kevin's phone number.

His buddy answered and put Kevin on, but when Charlotte explained that Pete didn't need him to come tomorrow Kevin said he would come anyway.

"But Pete doesn't think he has it in his budget to pay you," Charlotte said.

"He doesn't have to pay me," Kevin answered.

Charlotte's stomach began to churn as she tried to guess what Kevin was up to.

"But it's a long way for you to drive, what with gas and all being what it is."

"I'm happy to come. If it doesn't make a difference, so be it, but if it helps a little it's worth it. Besides," he said, "the kids are really warming up to me. Things are going great with them." Kevin said he'd be out by nine and then said good-bye.

Charlotte wrote herself a note on the pad beside the phone to call Marcus Lindstrom in the morning, not that she wouldn't remember. Kevin's words of enthusiasm about the kids were ringing in her ears and probably would all through the night. She'd put off calling their lawyer long enough.

TWENTY MINUTES LATER, after she'd folded a basket of towels and unloaded the dishwasher, she checked on Emily at the computer.

"I'm just working on my conclusion," she said.

Charlotte sat down in her chair and picked up her embroidery.

"Aunt Dana said we could write an essay about one of the characters in the novel, so I chose Boo Radley—how his dad's reaction to him shut him down, but how he still had a lot to offer the community."

"That sounds good," Charlotte said, working her needle through the fabric of the baby sheet. She'd decided on a frog pattern to go with the afghan Hannah was making.

"Boo's story makes me think of other people, how their past affects the way they act now."

Charlotte nodded. "Are you thinking about anyone in particular?" Charlotte asked. It sounded as if Emily was developing sympathy for Isabella.

"Actually..." Emily stared at the screen. "I was thinking about Dad."

Charlotte put her embroidery in her lap and turned her eyes toward her granddaughter. Emily met her gaze.

"Sometimes I wonder what my life would be like if Dad had had a good childhood. You know? Would he have been a good husband and dad? Made everything work?"

Or not run off with Denise in the first place? Charlotte scooted forward in her chair. *But then Sam, Emily, and Christopher wouldn't exist, and she absolutely could not imagine her life without them. That was just one of the many paradoxes of life.*

"Maybe Mom would still be alive."

"Those 'maybe' questions in life can eat away at us if we let them," Charlotte said.

Tears pooled in Emily's eyes. "Why do things have to be so hard?"

Charlotte stood and put her hands on Emily's shoulders. "That's the way life is," she said. "Life is hard and wonderful all at once, and sweetie, everyone is broken, not just your dad. But the thing is, God can use all of us—even though we're not perfect—to do his work."

"Like he used Boo Radley?" Emily turned back to the computer screen.

Charlotte chuckled, remembering that they were talking about a fictional character. "Yes, I think that's exactly what Boo represents. Often God uses the people we think are the least likely to have anything to offer."

Emily wrinkled her nose but didn't respond as she turned back to the screen and started typing again.

Charlotte yawned. "I'm going to bed. Don't stay up too late."

Emily nodded. "I'm almost done—and besides, Sam keeps bugging me for the computer."

"Where is he?"

"Out on the front porch, on his phone."

Charlotte started for the hallway. The reception was better outside than in the house. She stood at the open screen for a moment, breathing in the clean, rain-rinsed air, listening for Sam's voice. As she stepped through the doorway she heard him say, "Maybe I'm not the best person for the job."

Charlotte froze.

"Talk to Russell about it 'cause you're right, this isn't working. Bye."

Sam stood and shoved his phone into his pocket.

"Everything all right?" Charlotte asked, startling Sam.

He stepped backward, bumping against the rail. "Yeah. No." He clapped his hands together. "Lyla—my boss—drives me crazy. She's on me about everything—the printers, the website, the software, the hardware. It's one thing after another."

Charlotte took a step closer to Sam. "Sounds frustrating."

Sam shook his head. "Grandma, don't do that."

"What?"

"That get-the-kid-to-keep-talking stuff. Just tell me that I'm a jerk, that it's my job, and I should just buck up and do it."

Charlotte smiled. "Okay."

"But the thing is," Sam said, "I don't think I'm qualified. I'm spending way too much time on it."

"Sometimes a new job takes extra time."

"But I still need to study."

"And your classes are your priority," Charlotte said.

"Lyla wants to meet with me and Russell and hash things out. She said maybe we can divide up the work—or something."

"That sounds like a good idea." It would be great if he could keep the tuition compensation, at least; otherwise he had resigned from his job at Bill's office prematurely. She turned toward the door. "I'm off to bed. Don't stay up too late."

Sam groaned. "I still have a ton of homework to do."

Charlotte started to say he should have started earlier but didn't. He was in college. He needed to figure this out on his own.

Chapter Twenty

Wednesday morning, as soon as the kids left for school, Charlotte dialed Marcus Lindstrom's law office. The receptionist put her on hold for ten minutes, so she busied herself by wiping down the counters and cupboard doors while she waited with the cordless phone wedged between her ear and her shoulder. Finally, Marcus came on the line. She explained that Kevin had been staying in Harding for the last two weeks, had found a job, and had been coming out to the farm quite often, but she didn't know what his intentions were.

"What can I do to protect our rights as guardians?" she asked.

"Has he said what his intentions are?" Marcus asked.

"Not exactly," Charlotte said.

"Until you know what his plans are, there isn't a lot you can do," Marcus said. "But my advice is to be warm to him. Don't give him any reason to feel threatened. Encourage him to have a relationship with you and the kids. Unless he's a threat to their well-being or a bad influence, it's what's best for all of you."

Marcus went on to ask a few questions about Kevin's status. When Charlotte said Kevin was driving an old car and that the job with the machine shop probably didn't pay much, he told her that chances were he just wanted to be closer to the kids. "It costs a lot to raise children," Marcus said.

Charlotte exhaled. Didn't she know it.

Marcus continued, "It doesn't sound like he's in a position to gain custody. I wouldn't worry about it at this point."

"When *would* you worry about it?" Charlotte asked, squeezing the cleaning rag.

"If he comes into money or saves enough to get into a house of his own. When he's been in Harding for several months instead of a couple of weeks."

Charlotte thanked him for his time and hung up the phone. She would try to do better when it came to Kevin.

THREE HOURS LATER she started across the pasture with Toby at her side, still thinking about Kevin and the children. Britney trotted toward her, and Stormy followed. The filly was over two years old now. Pete and Emily could start breaking her to ride in the spring. Charlotte held out an apple for the mare, and Britney neighed, tossing her head. "Come on, girl," Charlotte coaxed. She held out another apple for Stormy.

The horses' noses were soft against her palms, and in a second the apples had disappeared. Charlotte rubbed each of their necks for a moment, and then they followed her as she continued across the pasture toward the soybean field. The morning had turned warm, and the sky was a bright, vibrant blue. As she approached the wire fence Toby began to bark. She glanced around, noting a decaying odor. Several yards to her left, toward the creek, was the carcass of another raccoon.

"Toby, no. Leave it alone," she commanded. The dog hesitated and then obeyed. Charlotte climbed over the fence. She could make out Kevin, bent over at the waist, in the middle of the field. Toby ran toward him, and he stood, spotted Charlotte, and waved. He wore a baseball cap and the white shirt he'd worn to church. Charlotte shuddered. It was going to be filthy, probably beyond ever coming clean.

Ahead were two bulging burlap bags. Kevin was really making progress.

She neared and called out, "It's time for lunch." She had determined to follow Marcus Lindstrom's advice.

"I brought a sandwich," he said, his hand on the bill of his cap.

"I thought so," Charlotte answered. "But I have pork chops, mashed potatoes, and coleslaw. And a peach pie for dessert."

Kevin grinned. "Guess I'd be crazy to settle for tuna."

Charlotte picked up one of the burlap bags, but Kevin took it from her and then grabbed the other one. As they started toward the fence, Pete called out, "Hey, wait!"

Charlotte turned. He was in his pickup, on the other side of the field.

"I can haul the bags," he yelled, leaning out the window.

Charlotte and Kevin changed directions and headed toward the road. Pete met them at the fence, took one of the bags, and then held the barbed wire down for Charlotte to climb through. Kevin tossed the other bag over the fence.

"I only have two rows to go," Kevin said, lifting one of the bags into the back of the truck. Pete unhooked the tailgate, and Toby jumped into the bed of the truck, leaping over the burlap bags to get closer to the window.

"I really don't think it's going to make a difference," Pete said.

"It might."

Charlotte climbed into the middle of the bench seat and then remembered the raccoon. "Pete," she said as he slammed his door. "There's another dead raccoon along the fence line of the pasture."

"I'll get it after lunch," he said.

"I can get it." Kevin took his hat off. "I saw it earlier and was going to mention it."

"I'll show you where the wheelbarrow and shovel are," Charlotte said.

As Pete started the truck, his cell phone rang. "Pete Stevenson," he said. He listened for a second and then mouthed to Charlotte, "It's the loan officer." He continued listening and then said, "You found it? Great."

There was another long pause on Pete's end. "It'd been saved with the real-estate loans?" And then, "Oh, sure, I understand that. I just need to know that you have it right now."

A minute later he said, "Yes. A short-term loan. Six months. It comes due in December."

Pete grinned. "Great. Fax me a copy, please, and put one in the mail too."

Charlotte was smiling too. "What a relief," she said.

Pete put his hand up and high-fived her, a little awkwardly but with gusto nonetheless.

"Hey," Kevin said. "Here comes Bob."

Sure enough, Bob's pickup raced toward them, bumping down the dirt road.

He opened his window and stuck his head out as he came to a stop, hood to hood with Pete's truck.

"Dana's at the clinic," he yelled. "The school secretary just called. She couldn't reach you on your cell." Then he backed up onto the edge of the field and turned around.

"Oh, dear," Charlotte said. "Do you want me to come with you?"

"No," he said. "I'll drop you off at the house."

"We'll ride with Dad," Charlotte said, and Kevin opened the door and stumbled out as Pete yelled for Bob to wait.

"Call," Charlotte yelled as Pete eased by Bob's truck and sped down the lane.

"**SOMETHING'S WRONG** with Mrs. Stevenson," Isabella said as she walked beside Emily to English class.

"No, she's fine." Emily was tired of Isabella's drama, making a big deal of Aunt Dana's being gone a few days.

"No, I saw her leave during lunch with Miss Carey. In Miss Carey's car. Mrs. Stevenson was walking funny, and she seemed upset."

"Maybe she didn't like the school lunch today." Emily certainly hadn't. She could barely stand the smell. It was some kind of stir-fry with pale vegetables and mystery meat. "She'll be in class. Just wait." Emily marched ahead. Grandma had said just last night that Dana was doing much better, that Dr. Carr said she was fine.

But when they shuffled into the classroom, Mr. Duncan was there, not Aunt Dana. Emily's heart raced. It must be serious to have the principal substitute for her.

"What's going on?" Isabella belted out.

"Mrs. Stevenson is ill." Mr. Duncan stood with his arms crossed, one big foot sticking out in front of him. "I'm going to fill in today." He glanced down at a piece of paper on the desk. "We're going to watch the film of *To Kill a Mockingbird*. The first part anyway. You'll watch the rest tomorrow."

"Will Mrs. Stevenson be back tomorrow?" Isabella asked, plopping down into her chair.

"I don't know." Mr. Duncan started to mess around with the DVD player under the TV. "Everyone move your desks forward," he said, "so you can see."

"Emily," Isabella's voice was loud. "Do you think she's pregnant?"

"I knew it!" Lily said as she came through the doorway, followed by Ashley. Lily slid into her desk. "Emily, when is she due?"

Emily put up her hands. "No one said she's pregnant."

"No one said she's not," Isabella retorted.

Emily tried to remember if Pete had talked about Dana while Isabella was in the field with them. She didn't think so. Emily shrugged as Ashley sat down beside her.

"Maybe Ms. Carey took her home because she has morning sickness."

"Or to the clinic," Lily said.

Emily gave Ashley a desperate look, and her friend chimed in, "Hey, who's going to the football game in River Bend on Friday?"

Lily was going, of course, because she was a cheerleader. Isabella said she would go if she could find a ride. Ashley said her dad was going and they had enough room for a couple of extra people. "Emily?" Ashley said.

"Huh?" She'd been listening; still, she was caught off guard.

"Want to go to the game on Friday?"

"Maybe."

Another wave of students, including Hunter, came in and scooted their desks forward as Mr. Duncan told the entire class that Mrs. Stevenson was ill.

"Pregnant," Isabella called out.

Mr. Duncan ignored her.

"Is she really?" Hunter asked, looking straight at Emily.

Emily slumped down in her chair. Everyone in school was going to know now.

Ashley cleared her throat as she raised her hand. "Mr. Duncan," she said, but she was looking straight at Isabella, "there seems to be a lot of speculation going on about a subject that isn't any of our business. Don't you think?"

His face reddened. "You're right, Ashley. Mrs. Stevenson's personal life isn't our business." He looked straight at Emily. "Well, it isn't for most of us. The subject is closed."

Emily mouthed *thank you* to Ashley. She could have hugged her. Next she glanced at Isabella. She slumped in her chair with a pout spread across her face.

Chapter Twenty-One

Pete sat in the chair beside the hospital bed, holding Dana's hand as the ultrasound technician slid the wand over her belly. He'd driven her from Bedford to the Harding hospital. There wasn't any reason for an ambulance because it wasn't a life-or-death situation, at least not one that anyone could do anything about. Still, Pete kept driving too fast, and Dana kept asking him to slow down.

Now they were in a little room with no windows, and Dana was wearing a hospital gown wadded up above her waist and a sheet pulled over her hips.

"What are you looking for?" Pete asked the technician.

"Shapes. And we can usually get a heartbeat by eleven weeks."

Dana kept her eyes on the screen, and Pete redirected his there too, not that he could make out anything except wavelike lines.

"Is that something?" Dana asked.

The woman nodded.

Pete wanted to ask if they would be able to tell if it was a boy or a girl, but then his eyes filled with tears and he had to look away and blink really hard. Somehow knowing what the baby was would make things harder if it didn't make it.

"Listen," the technician said.

Pete didn't hear anything.

The woman moved the wand around in the puddle of gel on Dana's belly.

"Do you hear that?"

Pete did. It sounded like the beating hooves of tiny horses. Dana smiled. She heard it too.

"It's the heartbeat," the technician said.

Dana reached for Pete's hand. "So it's okay?"

The technician kept her eyes on the screen. "The doctor will talk to you in a little while." The woman wiped off the wand and put it on the tray beside the machine. "Would you like a picture?"

"Of course." Dana sat up, leaning on her elbow.

The technician hit a button, and the machine made a whirring noise. She handed Dana a picture and then two more. "For the grandparents," she said and smiled.

Thirty minutes later they waited for the doctor in an exam room of the clinic across the street. "How are you feeling?" Pete asked, sitting on the stool.

Dana reclined on the examination table. "That's the third time in ten minutes you've asked me that." Her eyes were closed.

"Oh." Pete spun around on the stool. Maybe the baby was going to be all right after all. He didn't want to get his hopes up, but he couldn't help it. When he picked up Dana at the clinic in Bedford, she said she was bleeding worse than she had been before, and he'd felt sure she was miscarrying, but now they'd just seen the baby and heard the heartbeat.

There was a quick knock on the door, and Dana said, "Come in."

A young doctor with curly red hair entered looking down at a chart. Dana sat up and shook the man's hand as he introduced himself as Dr. Jones and said the doctor Dana had seen for her first prenatal visit was delivering a baby. Pete stood and shook the doctor's hand too and then stood on the other side of Dana.

"The ultrasound looks good," the doctor said, sitting down on the stool. "The heartbeat is steady, and the blood flow from the placenta is good. Eleven weeks is too early to make out much else." He smiled.

"What about the bleeding?" Dana asked.

Dr. Jones rolled toward the table. "Have you been doing a lot of lifting?"

Dana shook her head.

"Exercising a lot?"

Pete shook his head.

"On your feet too much?" the doctor asked.

"I'm a teacher."

"That could do it." Dr. Jones closed the file. "Obviously you've been worried about a possible miscarriage and with good reason. Bleeding sometimes means a miscarriage is imminent, but only half the time. The other half it's because of other things—and being on your feet too much is one of them."

Pete took a breath for what felt like the first time in three hours.

"Can you sit down to teach?" Dr. Jones asked.

"Sure," Dana said.

"Plan to stay off your feet as much as possible for the next two weeks. Of course, if you have heavy bleeding or cramping, get back over here. But if the bleeding stays light, give it some time." He stood. "What will be will be." He shook hands with both of them, said good-bye, and stepped into the hall.

Pete sat down on the edge of the table and put his arm around Dana. "Maybe things are going to be okay." He kissed her forehead.

Dana leaned against him. "It will be. I'm sure of it." She smelled like soap and chalk and sweetness. "Hand me my purse, would you, please? I want to look at the picture again."

"It's going on the fridge as soon as we get home," Pete said, smiling as he swung her purse forward. "Your mom will go crazy over this."

Dana pulled out the picture. "Your mom will too," she answered.

"I know," Pete answered, although Mom's "crazy" looked nothing like Bonnie's.

Dana held out the photo, and they both stared. "Look, she has your ears," Dana joked.

"Better than my balding—" Pete chuckled. "Oh, no. He has that too."

"He. She." Dana scooted to the edge of the table.

"It doesn't matter, does it?" Pete said.

"No. I just want this baby, more than I've wanted anything in my entire life." Dana's brown eyes brimmed with tears.

"Me too, next to you." Pete took her elbow and helped her stand, even though it wasn't necessary. "How about if I carry you to the car?"

"Pete."

"And how about if you don't go to school for the rest of the week?" He acted like he was going to pick her up, and she brushed him away.

"The doctor said to sit at school—not skip it." Dana stood and slung the strap of her purse over her shoulder.

"But we don't want to take any chances." Pete held his hat over his heart.

"But I don't want to use up my time now. I want to save it for when the baby's born."

"But we want the baby to be born. That's the point, right?"

Dana opened the exam room door and stepped into the hall. "Pete, I'll sit. I'll rest. But you heard what the doctor said—what will be will be. We have to trust God."

Pete followed her down the hall. "What will be will be" was hard to swallow when their baby was the subject, but the doctor and Dana were right. It was the same thing with the farm. And the house. He had to stop running around like a chicken with its head cut off and remember that the loan had worked out; the other stuff would too. If there wasn't anything he could do to change the outcome of something, then he had to trust God. He didn't have any other choice.

SAM HURRIED into the newspaper lab, out of breath from running up the stairs. Russell sat at the first computer.

"Hey," Sam said, "is Lyla in her office?" He was prepared to go get her so they could get started. The sooner they were done the better.

Russell shook his head without looking up. "She's late. As usual. So are you."

"I had to talk to my comp prof." He'd gotten a big fat C on his essay. He was allowed one rewrite for the term and couldn't decide if he should take it now or save it for later. He was inclined to wait just in case things got worse.

Sam peered over Russell's shoulder. "Hey, what are you doing?"

"Cleaning up the website. The archives were all messed up. The link to the volleyball team's article didn't work. And you messed up the editor's letter. That would really tick Lyla off."

Sam slumped down into a chair. "Thanks."

"So how much experience do you have with websites?"

"None," Sam muttered. "I can keep the printers going and the hardware, but I'm not doing so good with the rest."

"Do you want to learn this stuff?"

Sam shrugged. The truth was, he didn't really care. He used to think that he wanted to work with computers and maybe he still would, doing something like writing software, but he wasn't enjoying updating the website; that was for sure.

"I kind of miss it," Russell said. "Not the hassles with the printer and that sort of thing. But I liked the web stuff." He pulled his MacBook out of his backpack.

"So did you do your stuff from home?" Sam asked.

Russell flipped open his lid. "Nah. I just got this."

"But you could now?" Sam sat up straighter.

"Yeah, I guess so." Russell logged onto the college site and typed in his password information as Lyla walked into the room with a container filled with salad.

"Hi, guys." She seemed to be in a good mood as she pulled a chair toward Russell with her free hand. "Is the meeting called to order?"

"It is now." Russell closed his laptop. "Unless someone else is coming."

Lyla shook her head and took a bite of salad. Russell slipped his laptop into his backpack.

"So," Sam said, looking straight at Lyla, "what's on the agenda?"

"You." She smiled and put her salad container on the table behind her. "I don't think you have as much experience as you said."

Sam felt his old defensiveness rising, but then Russell caught his eye and smiled, and Sam relaxed a little. "Yeah. I kind of misrepresented myself. I thought I could pick it up as I went." Sam shrugged.

"Yeah, well, good intentions won't keep the newspaper going," Lyla said. "We've lost a lot of time. I need someone who knows this stuff, not someone who needs to be trained."

"My bad," Sam said.

Lyla's voice softened. "Not all your bad. I was desperate and pressured you into it." Her eyes were sincere. "Russell, are you sure you won't help us out again?" Lyla was practically begging.

"How about if we rearrange everything?" Russell suggested. "I do the website and the troubleshooting, and Sam does the maintenance stuff on the hardware."

Sam nodded. He could do that. It would mean less money though.

"And," Russell stood, "Sam takes over the advertisement sales."

"What?" Sam looked from Russell to Lyla.

"I got that sale at the mall because of you. All of the kiosk business people thought it was a great idea."

"I've never done sales," Sam said.

Lyla laced her fingers together and stretched them over her head. "Would you give it a try?" she asked. "Go out tomorrow and the next day? See how it goes? Because if that works, we could keep the money the same."

Sam's eyes widened. "Would I be paid on commission for the ads? I mean, would it be based on how many I sell?"

Lyla shook her head. "Nope. You're required to put in ten hours a week—right, Russell?"

"Yep."

Sam smiled, trying not to look too excited about the prospect. In that case, the time commitment wouldn't be the same at all; he'd be spending far less time selling ads than he'd been spending on the website stuff. "I'm game," Sam said. "As long as you load the paper in the printer, Lyla."

She held her fork in midair. "Touché," she said and then laughed.

Russell began digging in his bag and pulled out a binder. "This is what you need to sell the ads." He thumbed through it, stopping at laminated sheets that showed ad sizes and prices. "And here's the receipt book," he said, flipping to the back. "Take it home and look it over, and then call me if you have any questions."

Sam took the binder and grabbed his backpack.

"Check in with me after you sell some ads tomorrow," Lyla said. "Let me know how it goes." She stood and patted his arm.

"Will do," Sam said. He started toward the door and then turned, intending to say thank you, but Russell and Lyla were looking at each other, and Sam suddenly felt uncomfortable, as if he were interrupting something. He hurried out the door and down the hall.

Chapter Twenty-Two

Charlotte had a head of lettuce, two cucumbers, a bunch of carrots, and eight zucchini in her basket as she moved on through the garden to the row of crookneck squash. The plants were humongous with basketball-size leaves spreading along the ground. She bent down and twisted a yellow squash off the vine, and then another; then she made her way to the tomato plants.

She wished she had asked Pete to call with news about Dana. He'd been gone for four hours now. *Dear Lord*, she prayed again, *please protect this new family*. Maybe she would call the clinic in a few minutes. She pulled a big red tomato from the vine. More had ripened in the last few days. With the weather staying warm, she might not end up with many green tomatoes this year.

Toby began to bark, and Charlotte turned toward the road. Sure enough, the school bus was slowing to a stop. She turned her attention back to the garden. There was nothing like sliced tomatoes with a little salt; she could eat them for breakfast, lunch, and dinner every day of the year if they grew all year. Last night had been much cooler than the previous nights, and they hadn't had a thunderstorm in a couple days. It wouldn't be long until the first frost fell.

With her basket full, she started toward the house, waving to Emily and Christopher as they walked toward her, Toby between them.

"How was school?" Charlotte called out.

Emily hurried forward. "What's going on with Aunt Dana?"

"I'm not sure, sweetie. Pete got a call to meet her at the clinic."

"And then they went to Harding. That's what Isabella heard."

"From whom?"

"Someone in the office told her."

Charlotte waited for Christopher and then turned toward the house with the children.

"Is the baby going to be all right?" Christopher asked.

"I'll call Pete's cell phone," Charlotte said. If he didn't answer, she'd call Dana's. If it were just her, she would pray and wait, but it was hard for the children. She took a deep breath. But they needed to learn to cope too. "How about if we pray for Dana and the baby right now?"

The children both nodded their heads, and they stopped in the driveway and joined hands while Toby stood beside Charlotte, her tail bumping against Charlotte's leg.

After Charlotte said, "Amen," Christopher pointed toward Kevin's car. "Is Dad out in the field?"

"He's been out there all day."

"Is it okay if I help him?" Christopher asked.

"After you have a snack."

As Charlotte and the children started toward the house, Christopher said that Justin wanted to help in the field after school. "But I told him Uncle Pete couldn't afford to pay him. Then he said he'd work for free—that was after he tripped me during PE."

"Isabella said the same thing, that she wanted to help." Emily opened the back door. "She said she liked hanging out with us."

"Could they help tomorrow?" Christopher asked.

"Are you sure?" Charlotte walked through the door as Christopher held it, concerned that he wanted to be around someone who treated him badly.

As the children ate apples and slices of cheddar cheese, Charlotte dialed Pete's cell phone. She stepped into the family room, not wanting to speak in front of the children in case the news was bad. She let it ring until the call started to go into voice mail, and then she hung up, ready to dial Dana's number just as Toby started to bark. Maybe Kevin was coming in from the field.

"It's Pete and Dana." Christopher was on his way from the kitchen window to the back door as he spoke. Emily jumped up from the table, nearly knocking over her chair as she followed him; Charlotte hurried out behind them.

Pete and Dana were both climbing out of Pete's truck, and Dana had something in her hand. "I have something for you, Grandma," she said. Her hair was twisted up on her head in a haphazard way and her white blouse was wrinkled, but she had a smile on her face.

"Is it the baby?" Christopher ran toward her.

They all gathered around Dana, and she handed the ultrasound photo to Charlotte. She could make out the black-and-white image of the baby's profile. Already the little one's face was obvious and the torso and even the outline of legs and feet. "Amazing," Charlotte said, one hand gripping the photo and the other over her heart.

"Let me see." Christopher took the photo and made a face. "I don't get it."

Emily leaned in. "No. Look, there's her head and body. Look, that little bump is her nose."

"Her?" Christopher blushed. "Can you tell it's a girl?"

"No," Pete and Dana said in unison and then laughed. "But they can tell that the baby is okay. The heartbeat is strong, and so is the blood flow from the placenta," Dana said.

"The little mama needs to take it easy though," Pete said. "She's been on her feet too much."

"I'll sit while I teach," Dana said. "But the doctor said chances are, everything is okay."

"What a relief," Charlotte said, hugging Dana and then Pete. "Can you come in? And get off your feet?"

"Thank you, but we need to get back into town. Mom's at Grandma Maxie's." Then she nodded at the print still in Emily's hand. "That one is for you guys."

"Cool," Emily said. Her voice was excited, but her face immediately became serious. "The kids at school—at least the girls—have guessed that you're pregnant."

Dana smiled. "That's all right. I'm ready to tell everyone. Even if something happens—" She paused and looked at Pete. "Even if we lose this baby, I would rather have everyone know ahead of time than find out afterward. Because at this point it isn't like we wouldn't want people to know that there was a baby." She paused for a second. "We'd need their support." She swallowed hard.

Charlotte hugged Dana again. "I know exactly what you

mean." Then she turned to Pete. "Speaking of that, have you told your Aunt Rosemary?"

Pete slapped his forehead in his overly dramatic way. "No. We'll go by there after we see Bonnie and Grandma Maxie."

"If Dana feels up to it," Charlotte said.

"I could take you home so you can put your feet up," Pete said. "Then I'll go by Aunt Rosemary's shop."

They called out their good-byes as Pete and Dana climbed back into the truck.

Emily sighed.

"What is it?" Charlotte asked.

"I thought it was going to be embarrassing to have Aunt Dana pregnant—you know, to have all the kids talk about it. But now I'm just so relieved that the baby is going to be all right."

Charlotte put her arm around Emily but didn't say a word. Emily just needed her to listen. Christopher yelled that he was going to the field, and Charlotte waved with her free hand.

AN HOUR LATER, Charlotte slid the chicken into the oven to bake and turned her attention to slicing the squash as Christopher and Kevin came through the back door.

"Dad wants to know when Sam will be home," Christopher said.

Kevin's head bobbed in agreement.

"I don't know." She found it amusing that Christopher was speaking for his dad. She glanced at the clock. It was 5:15. "He should be home by now."

"I haven't seen much of him," Kevin said. "I thought if he was around, it would be nice to say hello before I leave."

"How about a cup of coffee while you wait?" Charlotte asked.

Kevin held out his dirty hands. "I'd better wash up first." He headed down the hall, and a second later, Bob sauntered into the kitchen, glasses perched on the end of his nose and the *Bedford Leader* in his hand. "Is he staying for dinner?" he whispered loudly.

Charlotte glanced around. Christopher must have gone into the family room. "I don't think so," she mouthed and then put her finger to her lips. Kevin had eaten lunch with them and it had gone well, but she was with Bob. She didn't want Kevin at every meal; it was too uncomfortable. But she didn't want to make a big deal about it in front of the kids.

Bob poured himself a cup of coffee and sat down at the table; a minute later Kevin joined him after Charlotte handed him a cup and the pitcher of cream from the refrigerator. Christopher hovered around, showing his grandfather and Kevin the photo of Pete and Dana's baby and then pulling out his homework.

"Have Grandpa help if you need it," Charlotte said.

Bob folded his newspaper and gave Charlotte a pathetic look as Christopher pulled his math book from his backpack.

"We're doing percentages," Christopher said. "If I spend eight hundred dollars a month on groceries and my income is sixty thousand dollars a year, what percentage of my money goes toward food?" he read.

"Eight hundred dollars a month?" Kevin hooted. "Who spends that much on groceries?"

Charlotte started to say she would spend that much and a lot more if weren't for the vegetables, eggs, milk, and meat the farm provided. If Kevin were interested in gaining custody of the kids she would be happy to bring him up-to-date on the costs.

"Christopher," Bob said, "what do you do first?"

Christopher tapped the eraser of the pencil against his lined paper. "Either I multiply eight hundred by twelve or divide sixty thousand by twelve." The kid really was good at math. A minute later Sam walked through the door with his backpack over his shoulder and a big white binder in his hand.

He said hello to everyone and then sat down at the table, opening the binder. "I might have a new job," he said, "selling ads for the newspaper."

"Besides the computer-support job?" Charlotte asked.

"Instead of part of that job."

"Sales?" Bob put the paper down. "That takes a lot of gumption."

"I think I'll like it," Sam said. "I start tomorrow. And I've been thinking about taking an Intro to Business class next semester."

"I've seen a few ads sold in my working days," Kevin said. "At the hardware store I worked at in San Diego. Even at the manufacturing place in Texas. I have an idea of what small business owners are looking for."

Sam pushed the binder over to his dad. "Do you want to take a look? See what you think? You might have some other ideas besides what's in here."

Kevin positioned the binder in front of himself and started reading.

"Sixteen percent," Christopher said. "Is that right?"

Kevin looked at Bob, who shrugged and then said, "Hold on a second." He tilted his head and worked through the problem. "Yep. That's right."

"Wow. Sixteen percent on food! It's a pity to spend all that money on something that doesn't last," Christopher said, "when you could be buying games and stuff like that."

"People have to eat."

"But that much?" Christopher slapped his forehead.

"Maybe it's a big family," Charlotte said.

"Yeah. A family of five," Bob added and then grinned.

Charlotte scooped the sliced squash into the frying pan. Yes, they were a family of five just trying to get by.

Thunder crashed in the distance, and Bob moaned as Charlotte let out a loud sigh. Here she thought the storms had ended. She shouldn't have been so optimistic; she knew there was no controlling the weather.

Kevin frowned. "I can come back tomorrow and pull more of the leaves."

"And Emily and I will help. Isabella and Justin too," Christopher said.

"Pete is going to have to finish seeding the winter wheat," Bob said.

"That's fine," Kevin said. "We can handle the fungus."

"I'm with Pete," Bob said. "I don't think it's going to make any difference either. And to be honest, I'm still not convinced it keeps coming on from the rain. I mean, the rain might be encouraging it, but—"

Charlotte shook her head. She didn't want the kids to

pick up on Bob's suspicions. "It can't hurt to pull the leaves," Charlotte said.

Bob was silent a moment and then said, "That's true. It can't." Then he turned toward Kevin, who was reading Sam's binder. "Would you like to stay for dinner?"

Kevin looked surprised. "I shouldn't. I've been imposing too much."

"Nonsense," Bob said. "It's the least we can do. You've been working in our fields. Of course we want to feed you."

AFTER DINNER, Charlotte pulled the plum crisp from the oven and placed it on the table. "I have ice cream for everyone but Grandpa," she whispered to Christopher. "Go get it from the freezer." She dished up Bob's serving first and put it in front of him.

Kevin began talking about selling advertisements as Charlotte passed the dessert around the table. "Sometimes you have to go back several times," he told Sam. "They want to get to know you. But you'll have an advantage being with a student publication. You would hope businesses would want to be supportive."

"I'm trying to think outside the box," Sam said. "I got the job because I suggested offering split ads to the kiosks at the mall. That way they could get an ad without having to pay as much."

"That's good thinking," Kevin said.

"So what exactly did you do in Texas?" Emily asked.

"Manufacturing—after I was laid off from the oil rig. For a family-owned place that made signs, but then the recession hit them hard and they had to let me go." He paused a second. "They had an eighteen-year-old daughter who graduated in the spring. She ran off to Florida last month with her boyfriend." He stopped, although he looked as if he wanted to say more.

"Did she come back?" Emily asked.

Kevin shook his head.

Charlotte stole a look at Bob, but he was concentrating on his dessert.

"That's weird," Emily muttered.

Charlotte thought Kevin might say more, but he didn't. He finished his crisp in silence and then told Sam he wished him well with his sales job.

"Thanks," Sam said. "I appreciate it."

Kevin left a few minutes later, saying he would see everyone the next day.

Christopher walked with him out to the car, but everyone else said good-bye at the back door.

"I don't get him," Emily said. "Not at all."

"We don't have to get him," Sam replied. "Maybe we can just let him be."

"Be what?" Emily turned on her heels. "Our dad? Or someone who just drops in and out of our lives?"

Sam shrugged. "Why don't you ask him what he plans to be?"

Emily looked like she was going to cry. "Why don't you? You're the oldest."

"I will," Charlotte said softly. "I'm sorry. I should have asked sooner. I'll ask him tomorrow what his plans are."

Chapter Twenty-Three

Emily slid into her seat in English class, and Ashley sat down behind her. Aunt Dana was at the back of the room, digging through a plastic box, but she started toward the front of the classroom as Isabella pranced into the room and sat in front of Emily. She turned around and whispered loudly, "Time for full disclosure."

Emily rolled her eyes.

"Oops," Isabella said. "I forgot my notebook." She turned toward Dana. "I'll be right back!"

"Boy, I wish she'd calm down," Emily whispered to Ashley.

"Could you at least try to be sympathetic?" Ashley's face reddened as she spoke.

"Huh?"

"I'm sorry," Ashley said, leaning closer. "But you've been on her since school started."

"But she's so annoying."

"She feels really vulnerable right now. Can you give her a couple more weeks until things settle down?" Ashley sighed. "I'm sorry. I didn't mean to jump on you. I just thought you'd be able to see through Izzy's pain."

"Class," Dana said as she walked toward the front of the room.

Ashley patted Emily's shoulder and then sat straight in her chair as Isabella came waltzing back into the room.

Hunter and his buddies took their seats behind Ashley as the bell rang, and Dana sat down in a chair in front of the chalkboard with a stack of papers in her hands.

She smiled at everyone. She wore makeup, her hair was twisted into a French roll, and the sleeves of her striped-blue blouse were buttoned at her wrists. Emily was sure she spotted a bulge under the stripes.

"I'm sorry I missed class yesterday. Mr. Duncan said you saw the first half of *To Kill a Mockingbird*. We'll watch the rest tomorrow." She glanced around the room, making eye contact with the students.

"I heard there's been some speculation about my condition, and I wanted to confirm that I am expecting a baby."

Isabella let out a hoot. "I knew it."

She turned around to Emily, her hand up in a fist bump, and Emily reluctantly responded. In the meantime Ashley gave her a gentle congratulatory pat on the back.

Dana continued. "There have been a few complications, but we're praying things are going to be fine. I need to be off my feet as much as possible."

Hunter's hand was up, waving back and forth.

"Yes, Hunter." Dana's eyes were smiling.

"May I pass out those papers for you—so you don't have to walk around?"

"Thank you." She held out the stack, and Hunter sprang to his feet. "I appreciate that." She faced the class again. "Your grades are on the back page for privacy."

Hunter scurried around the room as if in a race to pass the papers out in record time.

"I'm impressed with your essays. Your responses to the themes of the novel were insightful," Dana said. "You grasped that the novel transcends issues of race—that it's about being human and treating people as individuals, not objects."

Dana started to stand and then chuckled and shifted in her seat. "Boy, it's hard to sit and teach." She inhaled and exhaled slowly. "For tomorrow, I want you to write a one- or two-page reflection on how you can apply what you've learned from the book to your own life."

"Sounds like youth group," Isabella whispered.

Emily ignored her.

"These reflections will be completely confidential—just between you and me—so put a cover page on your paper to keep it private. It's due tomorrow."

Isabella groaned dramatically.

Hunter handed Emily her paper as Dana said, "Now, let's discuss the last chapter of the novel."

She started to stand, but Hunter called out, "I'll get it." He darted to Dana's desk and grabbed the book, handing it to her in a flash.

"Could you get my notebook too, please? It's the green one."

Hunter grabbed it and handed it to Dana and then finished passing out the papers as the discussion began.

Emily stared at the last page of her essay. There was a big A at the bottom of the page. Maybe Aunt Dana didn't expect more out of her than anyone else. She smiled for half a second and then frowned. She had no idea what she was going to write her reflection on.

AFTER LUNCH, Emily, Isabella, and Ashley sat on the bench under the big-leaf maple tree in front of the school. The umbrella of leaves was just beginning to turn yellow.

Troy stopped on the sidewalk and waved. Emily smiled.

"I heard you're going to have a new cousin," he said.

She nodded.

"Congrats," he said, as a group of guys at the edge of the school lawn called out to him. He waved again. "I'll catch you at your locker after school."

Emily nodded. Everyone was so excited about the baby, even Troy. She'd been ridiculous to think it would be an issue.

Isabella was talking, as always. "So now my grandparents are looking for a house in Bedford," she said, playing with the shoelace of her pink Converse. "They're looking at Mrs. Stevenson's house this afternoon."

"Really?" Emily's eyebrows rose. That would be great for Dana and Pete. For the whole family.

"They want to be closer to Justin's family. To help out."

"How come?" Emily asked.

"It turns out my aunt has chronic fatigue syndrome. She had cancer a few years ago and beat that, but her health hasn't been good since."

"Oh." Emily sat up straighter.

"How's your dad doing?" Ashley sounded concerned as she addressed Isabella, and Emily knew her friend was sincere.

"He had his hearing yesterday. He can't drive for six months, has a fine to pay, and is on house arrest for six months of weekends. Mom won't tell me how much the fine is."

Emily stared at the ground. *Probably because she knows you'll tell the entire town.*

"I'm sorry," Ashley said.

"I guess that's how things go. The really big bummer is that we're moving to Harding."

"What?" Ashley said and Emily echoed her, surprised that she sincerely meant it.

"We're going to move into Grandma and Grandpa's house. Isn't that a scream? It makes sense though. Mom's job is in Harding, and so is Dad's now. And since he can't drive, it's not like he can commute." Isabella's eyes sparked. "I asked if I could live here with Grandma and Grandpa, but Dad said I needed to be with them; but I'm hoping they'll let me come back for my senior year."

"Wow," Emily said.

"I guess you know what it's like to have your dad ruin your life, huh, Em?" Isabella said.

It was the first time the girl had called her Em, and it caught her off guard. "Kind of," Emily answered. Mom's dying was what had really messed up her life. She wanted to tell Isabella that things would work out, but it sounded trite.

"When are you moving?" Ashley asked.

"By the end of the month. That's when our lease is up on the apartment. I'll be staying out at my aunt and uncle's house part of the time until then."

The bell rang, and as the girls stood, Ashley gave Isabella a hug. "I'm sorry," she said. "I'm really going to miss you."

Emily hugged Isabella next but didn't say anything.

"Are we still on to work in the field today?" Isabella asked.

"Yep," Emily responded. "That's the plan."

CHARLOTTE, BOB, PETE, and Kevin sat at the picnic table on the porch and ate their turkey sandwiches with lettuce, tomato slices, and last year's pickles.

"I can't find any spots in the middle part of the higher field," Kevin said. "Just in a few rows on the outside."

Pete tilted his head like he didn't believe him.

"I'm serious. The kids and I should finish it after school."

Pete said he would take a look after lunch and then thanked Kevin. "You've really put in a lot of time. It really is working; I'll pay you."

Kevin shook his head. "I'd rather you didn't."

The conversation turned to the thunderstorm the night before and then to Pete and Dana's house in town.

"The Realtor is showing it this evening," Pete said. "Boy, it sure would be nice to pay what we can on the new house and finish up the financing. The contractor was out this morning and was putting up the outside walls, but I asked him to stop until everything works out."

Bob stood and said he needed to do some work on the combine, and Pete said he needed to get back to the seeding. Kevin followed Charlotte into the house, carrying a stack of dirty plates.

Charlotte thanked him as she took the stack and began rinsing them.

"I'll get back out to the field," Kevin said. "But I plan to meet the kids off the bus."

"I'll have a snack for them," Charlotte said. "And then you can all go out to the field together." She dried her hands on the towel as he headed to the door. She had to ask him. "Kevin," she said.

He turned around.

"I need to ask you something—straightforward." She stepped toward him.

"Okay." His voice was a little shaky.

"I've been beating around the bush about this when I shouldn't have been. I know you want to see the kids and all of that, but all of us need to know exactly what your intentions are."

"What?"

"Your intentions. Concerning the kids. What is your long-term plan?"

"Long term?"

Charlotte nodded. "The next few months. The next year."

"Whoa." Kevin stepped back. "Could we take this a little slower?"

Charlotte crossed her arms. "I'll be blunt. Are you going to seek custody?"

Kevin backed up and bumped into the wall. "Custody? No."

He didn't want custody. Charlotte's voice softened. "Then why did you come back?"

He didn't answer for a moment and then said, "Two reasons. One was that I saw what my employer went through when his daughter ran off, and I thought of you and Bob. I never thought of it from your perspective before." He looked her in the eye. "I'm sorry."

She nodded. She could accept his apology even though she couldn't speak at the moment.

"And I thought about the kids growing up. Sam will be the age I was when I went to San Diego soon. And in another two years Emily will be Denise's age. I've missed so much." He hung his head.

Charlotte stepped forward and touched his shoulder, the way she would have touched Sam's when he was out of sorts when they first arrived. "I'm glad you came back, Kevin," she said. "As long as the kids want to see you, we're not opposed."

"Thank you." He turned quickly and slipped out the door.

Charlotte grabbed a tissue, dabbed at her eyes, and sat down in her chair. Kevin didn't want custody, and he had empathy for what she and Bob had gone through. After obsessing day after day about what he was up to, she finally felt free. She dabbed at her eyes again. All she'd needed to do was ask.

Later that afternoon, as she vacuumed, she found herself humming hymns. And later still, as she folded clothes, she prayed for each of the children and then for Kevin. Not once did an imaginary conversation start playing in her head.

ISABELLA HAD NO SHAME; Emily was sure of it. She was prattling on about her dad as they worked their way through the field. "His lawyer said he was lucky," she said, talking to Dad. "It could have been a whole lot worse. The lady he hit is recovering. Plus he pleaded guilty right away so the judge was easier on him."

Dad said something in reply, but Emily couldn't hear him. She was pretty sure Isabella couldn't either. "The thing is that I didn't even know he still drank, but it turns out he had a problem. Mom's relieved he got caught—and that the woman he hit is okay. He started going to AA again. He said there are all these steps he needs to go through, including making amends. His sentence is part of that, but he needs to make amends to Mom and me too, and to Mom's parents. He said he broke all of our trust."

Dad was looking uncomfortable, but Isabella didn't seem to notice. "Hey," she continued, without taking a breath, "I think your job might be at the place Dad is working. Is your job at that factory right outside of Harding?"

Dad nodded.

"I think *my* dad getting a job there is why *you* ended up starting a week later. The owner is a good friend of my grandpa's."

Dad's eyebrows shot up.

"Anyway, my dad's name is Hank. I think you'll like him. Maybe you can give him a ride or something."

"Sure." Dad finally got a word in. "I'll look for him."

Emily kept her head down as she worked, hoping Isabella wouldn't keep talking.

"Hey, knock it off." Christopher's voice came from a row over.

Emily stood, straightening her back slowly, just in time to see Justin lob a dirt clod at Christopher. Her brother put his forearm up and blocked it.

"Knock it off, Justin," Emily growled.

The boys went back to work, and Isabella stayed silent as they made their way down the rows.

"I think this is helping," Dad said. "I couldn't find any new fungus on the leaves where we already worked the field."

"Cool," Emily said.

"Em."

Emily bristled at her dad being so familiar. She looked toward him, her eyes hard.

"Your grandmother and I had a good talk this afternoon. I told her I came back to the area to be able to see all of you." He coughed a little. "I guess I have some amends of my own to make. But I'm not here to get custody or anything. I can see Heather Creek Farm is a good place for all three of you."

Emily nodded but didn't say anything. She glanced at Isabella, who was about ten yards ahead and singing to herself. Emily avoided looking at her father, afraid she might smile. The relief she felt nearly made her laugh. For the first time, she could imagine asking him about his life. Not today. But sometime.

She'd been reading her Bible at bedtime since Ashley shared her life verse in English class. Not every night, but a few times a week. She was working her way through Psalms, and the passage she read last night talked about God's loving-kindness. She liked thinking of the two words together. She was feeling that right now: loving-kindness. That's what benevolence was all about.

AN HOUR LATER, as they made their way back to the house, Toby ran circles around Christopher as he dragged his burlap bag of soybean leaves.

Justin picked up a stick and threw it to the dog, and when Toby brought it back, dropping it at Justin's feet, he picked it up and poked her with it. Toby yelped.

"Knock it off," Christopher said.

Justin shook his head and laughed, poking at Toby again. She shied away.

"Don't mess with her," Christopher said, lunging for the stick, but Justin put it behind his back.

Christopher's face reddened; it looked like he was doing everything he could to control himself. Emily stepped forward, but Dad caught her arm and stopped her. "Let him figure it out," he said, but then he turned to Christopher and said, "Toby is important, and so are you."

Christopher turned toward Justin. "No more," he said.

"No more what?" Justin didn't move.

"No more teasing my dog and no more bullying me."

"Bullying? Who? What are you talking about?"

Dad nodded. "Yes, Justin, that's what you've been doing. That's what we've been telling you to stop doing all week."

Justin dropped his head.

Christopher started running across the pasture with Toby racing after him. He stooped and grabbed a stick and threw it, chasing after the dog as she sprinted ahead.

"He's the weirdest kid I've ever met," Justin said.

"And you're the meanest." Isabella sang her words in a faux opera style.

Justin covered his ears. "Stop that."

The two girls picked up their pace, but Kevin waited for Justin and walked beside him. Emily would tell Christopher about Justin's mom later; it helped her understand Justin to know that he had worries at home. It always helped to know what someone else's story was.

Isabella's pink shoes were covered with dirt. She said she would just wash them, but Emily was sure they would be stained. Suddenly Emily felt an ache in her heart. Isabella was loud and obnoxious and gossipy, but she was also honest and compassionate and caring. She would miss her, for sure. She had wanted her to be something different—to not butt in, to not be so intense, to not ask so many questions. But Isabella was who she was. And Ashley was correct; right now the girl was really vulnerable.

Emily caught up with her friend. That was what Dana had been talking about all along in class. It wasn't a life-or-death issue like in *To Kill a Mockingbird*, but it was a human issue. She hadn't accepted Isabella for who she was.

Dad and Justin trailed behind them. She knew the people she needed to write about in her essay—Dad, Justin, and Isabella. She'd judged them without knowing their stories. She felt a wave of disappointment in herself. She, of all people, should have known better. *Now you know*, she said to herself, parroting Grandma's words. *Move on.*

Chapter Twenty-Four

Charlotte filled the carafe with coffee and then started another pot. Pete had called a meeting of the neighboring farmers and she wanted to have something to serve. Hannah was coming with Frank and bringing her famous cinnamon rolls.

Pete was relieved last night when he walked through the fields. He hadn't found a single leaf with the fungus on it.

The front doorbell rang, and Charlotte started down the hall. Only Silas Maynard used the front door. It had to be him. She opened the door. In front of her stood a tall, thin man wearing a work shirt that had a Brask Farms insignia on the pocket. "Hello," he said. "I'm Slim Stanton, the foreman at—"

"Brask Farms," Charlotte said. "Come on in."

"Is Pete here?" He stepped into the entryway.

"He'll be right in. Come sit in the living room." She closed the door and led the way, wondering what Pete was up to. Just as Slim settled onto one of the folding chairs the front bell rang again.

"Excuse me." Charlotte hurried to the door. This time it was Silas Maynard, standing with his straw hat in his hands. "Morning, Charlotte," he said.

"Come on in, Silas." She swung the door wide. "Slim Stanton from the corporate farm is here."

Silas took a step forward and then stopped in his tracks. "Say what?"

"You heard me," she whispered. "He's in the living room, so behave yourself."

Silas sputtered a little and then followed her. As he plopped down on the couch she said, "I'll be right back with coffee."

"A little cream, please," he said.

"I remember," she responded. "How about you, Slim?"

"Black, thank you."

Slim asked Silas how he'd been as she hurried into the hall. He seemed like a nice man, like regular folk.

As she entered the kitchen, Hannah and Frank came through the back door, followed by Pete and Bob and then Ken Driggers and Walt Freeman.

Charlotte whispered to Pete that Slim Stanton was in the living room, and he smiled, rubbed his hands together, and told everyone to grab a cup of coffee and head to the living room. Hannah served the cinnamon rolls onto individual plates and carried them in three at a time, and Charlotte followed her with coffee for everyone.

Pete was introducing Slim to the other men when Charlotte handed the newcomer his coffee. He made eye contact with her and smiled as he said, "Thank you."

"I'm going to be direct," Pete said. "I've put a lot of thought and prayer into this, and that's why I asked Slim here." He remained standing and spoke to Slim. "There's been some speculation that since we all have the fungus and you don't that perhaps you might somehow be responsible for it."

Slim remained calm. It was obvious that Pete had briefed him on the situation. "I can understand that it might seem suspicious," he said, "but I can assure you that we would never do something like that. It would be unconscionable. And besides, when would we have the time? We just purchased a small parcel down the road—out past your way, Mr. Driggers—so that's why you've seen our trucks on the highway."

Silas Maynard cleared his throat. "So you're set on stealing more of our land."

"Oh, no," Slim said. "We're maxed out. And in fact we didn't pursue this last tract; they came to us, asking if we would buy it."

"Any other questions?" Pete looked around the room.

Bob's face was slack. Charlotte couldn't even guess what he was thinking.

"Well I think we can beat this," Pete said. "We've almost stopped it here. One person working one more day should finish it. We could go through Frank's field tomorrow and then all work together on Silas's."

"So the research assistant at Harding College was right after all," Frank said.

"She gave us good advice." Pete put his coffee cup on the end table and cut a bite of cinnamon roll with his fork. "But it's been the kids helping that has made the difference —the kids and Kevin."

"Kevin?" Silas Maynard had a confused look on his face.

"Sam, Emily, and Christopher's dad," Charlotte explained.

"Well, I'll be," he said.

"If you want to hire him he'd probably take you up on it. He's done wonders in our field."

"I'll think about it," Silas said.

"In the meantime, we'll stick to our plan and trust God with the rest," Pete said, his mouth half full. "I'll check the moisture in our crop tomorrow, and if it's close to twelve percent, I'll start harvesting early next week." He nodded toward Hannah. "This is even better than I remember."

Slim murmured in agreement as he took the last bite of his cinnamon roll.

Bob put his coffee cup down and leaned back in his chair, his hands wrapped around his knee. He had a mysterious smile on his face.

As the men finished their coffee, the phone rang. Charlotte was going to let it go to voice mail but then thought it might be Dana. She hurried into the kitchen and picked up the phone.

It was Randy, Pete and Dana's Realtor. "I hate to bother Pete while he's working," he said. "I know how busy he is, but I wanted to let him know we have an offer on the house, and I couldn't get through on the cell."

"I'll go get him," Charlotte said, walking toward the living room. She put her hand over the receiver. "Pete," she said quietly, "it's the Realtor."

Pete stood up, quickly juggling his plate as he grabbed the phone, and then hurried into the hallway.

The other men finished their coffee. "Well, I didn't really believe it was you," Silas said with a laugh as he reached out to shake Slim's hand. "But it makes me feel better to know for sure just in case I have to sell out to you in a few years."

"Like I said," Slim said, "we're maxed out." He laughed. "You'll have to sell out to some other corporate farm."

"Don't talk that way," Bob said.

"Yeah," Hannah said as she collected plates. "Pete's going to buy us all out—right, Charlotte? And we can all live it up at Bedford Gardens on the money we make off the sales."

Charlotte smiled. She planned to die at Heather Creek Farm with her grandchildren—and great-grandchildren—around her. "I'll come visit you," she said to Hannah with a sassy smile. This meeting with the neighbors was much more relaxed than the first one, and it had been brilliant of Pete to invite Slim. Charlotte offered up a silent prayer of thanks that God had led them to the best solution.

"All joking aside, Pete's done a good job," Silas said. "I've had my doubts about him through the years, but he's turned around. He's a good leader. And a hard worker."

Bob hooked his thumbs into his suspenders. "I think so too," he said. "He's proven himself to be a leader—both in the family and in the community."

A few minutes later Silas slipped out the front door, followed by Slim, who was followed by Ken Driggers and Walt Freeman, who were peppering him with questions about the operation.

Bob and Charlotte walked Hannah and Frank to the back door.

"Tell Pete thank you," Frank said. "I'll start working around the perimeter of the field, but if he has extra hands that would be a great help."

"I'll tell him to call," Charlotte said.

As she closed the back door, Pete let out a whoop in the kitchen.

"We have an offer," he said. "It's a good one, and the buyers are in an excellent financial position."

"That's good to hear, son," Bob said.

Charlotte gave Pete a hug. "Congratulations!"

"They want to sign next week."

"That soon?"

"That soon..." Pete's voice trailed off. "That means we're going to have to pack and move in with Grandma Maxie. We're going to need help."

"You've got it," Bob said.

Pete slapped his hand on his leg. "I better finish seeding the winter wheat." He started for the door but turned. "Is Kevin coming this morning?"

"He should be here any minute."

"Oh, good," Pete said. He stood still now, next to his dad. "Mom, could we have a family dinner tonight—say, out at the new house? We could picnic on the floor. Maybe Bill and Anna and the kids could come."

"And Bonnie and Grandma Maxie?"

"That would be great," Pete said. "And Kevin," he added.

Charlotte nodded in agreement. "I'll make fried chicken and potato salad. And a couple of pies." And lots of fresh veggies.

"Perfect," Pete said. "I'll be back for lunch. If Dana can't reach me on my cell, she's going to call the house to tell me how she's feeling."

SAM FLIPPED to the next page of the binder, the one with samples of the newspaper. "College students practically live on pizza," Sam said, looking up and making eye contact with the manager of Pino's, the place where he'd eaten last Friday night with Lyla and her group.

"You're right," the man said. "I don't know why no one's been in here to sell me an ad before."

"Do you have a lunch special?" Sam asked.

"No, but I could come up with one."

"That might be good for the ad because you're within walking distance of campus," Sam said, "and within easy driving distance. Students are always looking for a quick, affordable lunch." He was careful not to use the word *cheap*. That was part of the training in selling the ads—use positive words.

"That's a great idea. When do I need to get the ad copy to you?"

Good question. Sam hesitated. It was Friday. "Next Tuesday," he said. "You can e-mail it. The address is on the contract. Or let me know if you need me to pick it up." He was certain everyone would use e-mail, but he thought offering to pick it up was a nice touch.

They talked size and then price, and twenty minutes later Sam left with a check in the pocket of the binder. It was his first try—and his first sale.

Five stops later he had three more sales. He pulled his car into the college parking lot. A couple of minutes later he was running up the stairs to the newspaper lab and then bounding through the door, but as he did his face reddened. Lyla and Russell were sitting in front of the computers, holding hands and looking into each other's eyes.

"Oh, hi." Lyla pulled her hand away, but she didn't seem embarrassed. "How are you?"

"Good. I made four sales."

"You're kidding!" Russell stood with his hand out for a high-five. Sam gave it to him, hard.

"Looks like it all worked out," Lyla said, tugging on the sheer blue scarf around her neck.

"When's the deadline for the artwork and copy?" Sam asked.

Lyla made a face and looked at Russell. "What did we decide?"

"I don't think we did." He shrugged.

"How about Tuesday? That's when I told everyone to e-mail it in by."

"Perfect," Lyla said. Then she smiled and did a little dance walk into her office.

Sam said good-bye to Russell and headed to the door and then stopped, turning around slowly. "So, what's up with you and Lyla?"

Russell smiled and then said, "Sorry, you kind of got dragged into the middle of our spat."

"So Lyla's that bad, huh?" Sam grinned.

"No." Russell laughed. "She's just intense." Russell folded his laptop. "Want to go out to pizza with us tonight? Same deal as last time."

Sam shook his head. He was anxious to get home and tell Grandma how things had gone. "But make sure and tell the manager you work for the newspaper. Tell him thanks for buying an ad."

"You sold him an ad?" Russell whistled. "I never once thought of selling to him. I told you I was a really bad salesman."

"Yeah, well, I was a really bad webmaster." Sam held his hand up to his mouth, as if he had told a secret. Then he laughed and headed out the door.

Chapter Twenty-Five

Charlotte loaded the foil-covered trays of fried chicken into the cooler and put the large metal bowl of potato salad on top. She had tablecloths, napkins, paper plates, cutlery, and cups already packed, along with the Crock-Pot full of baked beans, all secured in a box in the back of Bob's truck.

"How's the lemonade coming?" she asked Emily.

"It tastes a little tart." Emily held the wooden spoon over the sink as she tasted it.

"It's perfect then," Charlotte answered. "Make sure the lid is tight and put it in the cooler on the table."

Charlotte pulled two big bags of sliced carrots, celery, and cucumbers from the refrigerator, admiring the photo of her newest grandchild as she closed the door.

The back door banged, and Christopher called out, "Uncle Bill and Aunt Anna are going on down to the new house."

"Thanks," Charlotte said. "Christopher, grab the folding lawn chairs off the porch, okay? All four of them. And tell Grandpa that you and he need to load the folding table."

It wouldn't do to have Grandma Maxie sit on the floor of the house with a cast on her leg, and Charlotte couldn't imagine Bob eating that way either. And of course Dana should have a chair to sit in too, and Bonnie. Chuck couldn't join them, unfortunately. He was on the road in Illinois.

Emily screwed the lids on both gallon jars of lemonade and put them in the cooler.

"Will your dad go down to the house or come back here first?" Charlotte asked.

"He wanted to get done as much as possible; he's nearly finished."

"I hope Sam is on his way home," Charlotte said. She'd forgotten that he'd gone out to pizza the Friday before and hadn't thought to leave him a voice mail about what the plan for the evening was.

"Want me to call him?" Emily asked, a tone of teasing in her voice.

Charlotte smiled and shook her head. "How was Dana today?"

"Fine. We watched the rest of *To Kill a Mockingbird* today. I really liked it this time."

"It's an amazing story," Charlotte said.

Emily hoisted the cooler off the table. "Grandma, what are God's commandments?"

"What do you mean?"

"I know the Bible is full of rules and stuff, but what are His commandments?"

Charlotte picked up the basket of food. There weren't that many rules, but she understood why Emily felt that way. "Well, Jesus said that the greatest commandment is to love the Lord your God with all your heart, soul, and mind, and the second greatest commandment is to love your neighbor as yourself."

"So, basically," Emily said as she nudged the back door open, "we're supposed to love God, others, and ourselves."

"Yep. Basically, that's it." It sounded so simple that Charlotte nearly started to laugh as they hurried along the walkway, aiming for Bob's pickup, which was parked with the tailgate open.

"I think I've found my life verse," Emily said.

"Really?" Charlotte hadn't known she was looking.

"Yeah. You know how Ashley's is Jeremiah something, that one that starts, 'For I know the plans I have for you?'"

Charlotte nodded. She remembered Emily talking about that weeks ago.

"Well, I was reading my Bible last night—Psalm 119."

Charlotte nodded. That was one of her favorite passages.

"It goes like this: 'I shall run the way of your commandments, for you will enlarge my heart.'"

"That's beautiful, Emily." Charlotte slid the basket onto the tailgate and then pushed it into the bed of the pickup.

"It's like, when I do the right thing, I feel my heart getting bigger; I have more love—more benevolence." Emily grunted a little as she pushed her cooler into the back of the rig.

They stepped back as Christopher and Bob came around the side of the house with the table.

Emily continued. "And I've been thinking about Atticus Finch, how he did the right thing even though most of the town was against him. That made his heart larger—made him able to do the right thing even more."

"You're right," Charlotte said.

"Grandma." Emily stepped away from the pickup. "I wish I had been a better friend to Isabella, more understanding."

"Now move on," Charlotte said.

Emily smirked. "You already said that in my head."

Charlotte stopped. "What?"

"I already imagined you saying that. And now, 'Move on.'"

Charlotte put her hand on Emily's shoulder. "It's true. You can still be a good friend to Isabella."

"I know." Emily's eyes were teary. "And I will. And I'm going to apologize to her for how I've acted."

ANNA AND BONNIE helped Charlotte arrange the food on the tailgates of Bob's and Pete's pickups. The plywood walls were up on the second floor and on three sides of the downstairs, but the front of the house was still open, defined by just two-by-four studs.

Bob and Pete set the table up in the future living room, and Emily spread the old tablecloths on the floor. Dana opened a lawn chair for Grandma Maxie to sit on and helped the older woman get settled. Then Dana sat in a lawn chair beside her. Christopher, Madison, and Jennifer ran up the stairs to the second floor as Bill scooped Will up off the floor before he could attempt the first step.

A car came down the drive, and Charlotte wondered if Kevin had decided to drive over, but she looked up and there was Rosemary, waving as she parked.

"Dana invited me," she said, grabbing a basket from the backseat. "I just happened to bake chocolate chip cookies last night to celebrate my being a great-aunt for the seventh time." She laughed. "Where's my walker?" She looked around. "I can hardly believe I'm still standing with that title."

Charlotte hugged her sister-in-law as they laughed together. Kevin arrived and washed his hands at the spigot on the side of the house just as Sam parked his car. Emily had sent him a text. Charlotte didn't ask if he'd waited until he got to the house to read it.

Then Pete called everyone together. "Dad," he said, "would you say a prayer?"

"Actually," Bob said, "I'd be honored to have you do that."

Pete seemed a little uncomfortable, but he managed a sweet prayer of thanks for the baby, for the house that was in the process of selling, for the new house, and for all the family. "Thank you for everything you've given us," Pete said, "including this soybean crop and all the hands that worked to save it."

A round of amens joined Pete's. As Christopher, Madison, and Jennifer darted toward the food, Bob boomed, "Hold on a second. I have an announcement to make."

The kids looked startled and scurried back to the adults.

"As you may know," Bob said, "I took over Heather Creek Farm when I married Charlotte. For a while now I've been trying to decide when was the best time to turn over the farm to Pete. Now I've decided," he said and then paused. "But first I have a confession to make." He turned to Pete. "I never believed Brask Farms sabotaged the crop." He grinned and then added, "I just joined in on the conspiracy theory to see how you would handle it, and I have to say, you exceeded my expectations."

"Dad!" Pete shook his head, and Bob grinned again, looking years younger for a moment.

Will started to squeal, and Bill handed him to Emily.

Bob continued. "And so, after we're done with harvest—after the soybeans and the corn and the wheat are all sold and the loan is paid off—Pete will become the official head of this farm."

Everyone clapped, and then Bob cleared his throat. "Pete's shown real leadership, but even more important, he's shown that he can trust the good Lord—not himself—to keep Heather Creek Farm running."

Pete's face grew red. "Thanks, Dad," he stuttered.

"I would like to stay on as head mechanic," Bob said, a twinkle in his eye, "so you won't be rushing out to buy a new tractor or anything."

Pete took his hat off and ran his hand through his thin hair. "Ah, Dad," he said. "That's the only reason I wanted you to retire." Then he chuckled. "Actually, I'm hoping you'll stay on as chief adviser."

Bob took a step forward, and Pete met him halfway. First they shook hands, and then Bob pulled him in for a hug.

Charlotte stepped back, tears in her eyes as she took in her growing family. She thought of two and half years ago, when Sam, Emily, and Christopher arrived in Nebraska, scared and full of grief. Each would have ongoing struggles, sure, but all three of them were moving forward, growing and flourishing. She wanted to raise these kids, wanted to see it through. All along she'd known she could trust God with their future, but looking around at all He had done these past few years, she knew that she had nothing to worry about. There may be hard days ahead, but they were all in God's hands.

Charlotte hugged her sister-in-law as they laughed together. Kevin arrived and washed his hands at the spigot on the side of the house just as Sam parked his car. Emily had sent him a text. Charlotte didn't ask if he'd waited until he got to the house to read it.

Then Pete called everyone together. "Dad," he said, "would you say a prayer?"

"Actually," Bob said, "I'd be honored to have you do that."

Pete seemed a little uncomfortable, but he managed a sweet prayer of thanks for the baby, for the house that was in the process of selling, for the new house, and for all the family. "Thank you for everything you've given us," Pete said, "including this soybean crop and all the hands that worked to save it."

A round of amens joined Pete's. As Christopher, Madison, and Jennifer darted toward the food, Bob boomed, "Hold on a second. I have an announcement to make."

The kids looked startled and scurried back to the adults.

"As you may know," Bob said, "I took over Heather Creek Farm when I married Charlotte. For a while now I've been trying to decide when was the best time to turn over the farm to Pete. Now I've decided," he said and then paused. "But first I have a confession to make." He turned to Pete. "I never believed Brask Farms sabotaged the crop." He grinned and then added, "I just joined in on the conspiracy theory to see how you would handle it, and I have to say, you exceeded my expectations."

"Dad!" Pete shook his head, and Bob grinned again, looking years younger for a moment.

Will started to squeal, and Bill handed him to Emily.

Bob continued. "And so, after we're done with harvest—after the soybeans and the corn and the wheat are all sold and the loan is paid off—Pete will become the official head of this farm."

Everyone clapped, and then Bob cleared his throat. "Pete's shown real leadership, but even more important, he's shown that he can trust the good Lord—not himself—to keep Heather Creek Farm running."

Pete's face grew red. "Thanks, Dad," he stuttered.

"I would like to stay on as head mechanic," Bob said, a twinkle in his eye, "so you won't be rushing out to buy a new tractor or anything."

Pete took his hat off and ran his hand through his thin hair. "Ah, Dad," he said. "That's the only reason I wanted you to retire." Then he chuckled. "Actually, I'm hoping you'll stay on as chief adviser."

Bob took a step forward, and Pete met him halfway. First they shook hands, and then Bob pulled him in for a hug.

Charlotte stepped back, tears in her eyes as she took in her growing family. She thought of two and half years ago, when Sam, Emily, and Christopher arrived in Nebraska, scared and full of grief. Each would have ongoing struggles, sure, but all three of them were moving forward, growing and flourishing. She wanted to raise these kids, wanted to see it through. All along she'd known she could trust God with their future, but looking around at all He had done these past few years, she knew that she had nothing to worry about. There may be hard days ahead, but they were all in God's hands.

About the Author

Leslie Gould is the #1 bestselling and Christy-Award winning author of over forty novels. She and her husband, Peter, live in Portland, Oregon and enjoy hiking, traveling, and hanging out with their adult children and young grandson.

A Note from the Editors

We hope you enjoyed this volume in the Home to Heather Creek series, published by Guideposts. For over seventy-five years, Guideposts, a non-profit organization, has been driven by a vision of a world filled with hope. We aspire to be the voice of a trusted friend, a friend who makes you feel more hopeful and connected.

By making a purchase from Guideposts, you join our community in touching millions of lives, inspiring them to believe that all things are possible through faith, hope, and prayer. Your continued support allows us to provide uplifting resources to those in need.

Whether through our online communities, websites, apps, or publications, we strive to inspire our audiences, bring them together, and comfort, uplift, entertain, and guide them.

To learn more, please go to guideposts.org.

Find inspiration, find faith, find Guideposts.
Shop our best sellers and favorites at
guideposts.org/shop
Or scan the QR code to go directly to our Shop